TOTAL FOOTBALL

Sanjeev Shetty is a sports journalist with nearly twenty years' experience. He works for the BBC as a producer and reporter on its international services covering its sports news channels. He is the author of *No Middle Ground* and *Messigraphica*. Sanj lives in Cheshire, UK, with his family.

TOTAL FOOTBALL

A GRAPHIC HISTORY OF THE WORLD'S MOST ICONIC SOCCER TACTICS

SANJEEV SHETTY

Aurum
Press

Brimming with creative inspiration, how-to projects and useful information to enrich your everyday life, Quarto Knows is a favourite destination for those pursuing their interests and passions. Visit our site and dig deeper with our books into your area of interest: Quarto Creates, Quarto Cooks, Quarto Homes, Quarto Lives, Quarto Drives, Quarto Explores, Quarto Gifts, or Quarto Kids.

First published in 2018 by Aurum Press
an imprint of The Quarto Group
The Old Brewery, 6 Blundell Street
London N7 9BH
United Kingdom

www.QuartoKnows.com

A catalogue record for this book is available from the British Library.

ISBN 978 1 78131 784 6

1 3 5 7 9 10 8 6 4 2
2019 2021 2022 2020 2018

Designed by Dave Jones
Illustrations by Fergus McHugh

Printed in China

CONTENTS

INTRODUCTION

The Chinese military strategist Sun Tzu (544–496 BCE) wrote that all warfare is based on deception. Perhaps the same could be said of employing tactics to win a game of football. Despite all the evidence that suggests one team is superior to another, football tactics – and the ways in which formations can vary because of them – explain why teams such as Barcelona and Manchester City never go a whole season undefeated.

But football is not a happy accident. Although this book charts tactics and formations from the 1950s onwards, there are references dating back to the 1930s, when the Austrian coach Karl Rappan was perfecting his 'bolt' philosophy. Eighty years ago, when radio was considered the most modern of innovations and televisions were not a household commodity, a coach was trying to shut the door on attacking play, using clipboards and words as his tools. What has happened since that time, is

that other coaches have taken Rappan's theories and perfected them, each of them developing a more sophisticated method. There is one certainty in life: although we keep improving on what we know, there is always someone around the corner who can take things even further.

While the desire to win is in our sporting nature, there is also an ambition to create something wonderful. The supreme Hungarian side of the 1950s was eventually superseded by Real Madrid's first great team, before the Brazilians gave us their version of the beautiful game. More recently, Pep Guardiola and his rebuilt Manchester City team have refined what we expect from title winners. It is not a case of putting together a group of well-paid players and hoping for the best – this team aims to thrill. There is mention of Guardiola's other great side – his Barcelona squad that dazzled between 2008 and 2012, but no specific chapter dedicated to a team developed by José Mourinho. That is not intended as a slight against the highly-successful Portuguese manager, nor other great coaches not featured within, but more a reflection of how football's moods and trends have been shaped by others.

The surety of football is that someone, somewhere, is conceiving of a plan to take on whoever happens to be the dominant side of the moment – that is the very nature of football when played at the highest level. And it is why football continues to be a mass of goals, tackles, tactics, formations, innovations, words and contradictions.

LINE-UP POSITIONS

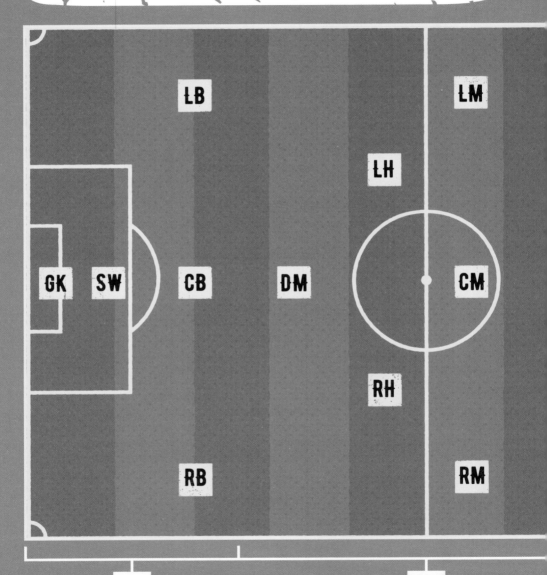

LB

LM

LH

GK SW CB DM CM

RH

RB RM

DF Defender

MF Midfielder

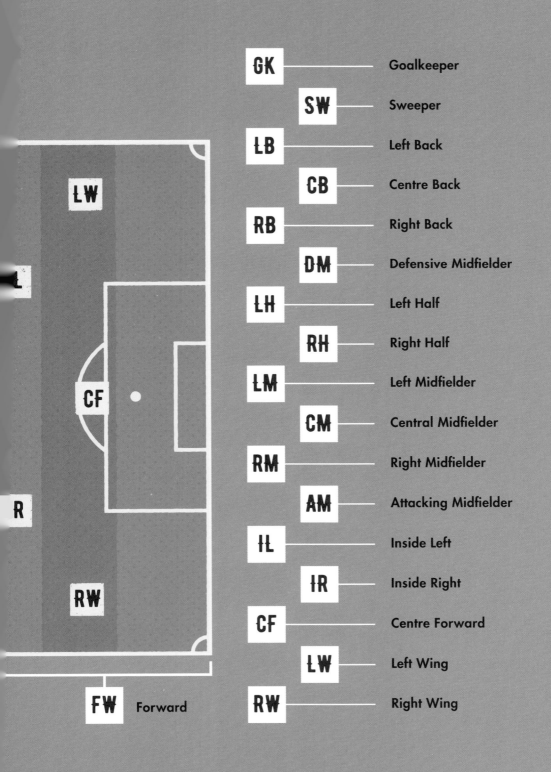

GK		Goalkeeper
	SW	Sweeper
LB		Left Back
	CB	Centre Back
RB		Right Back
	DM	Defensive Midfielder
LH		Left Half
	RH	Right Half
LM		Left Midfielder
	CM	Central Midfielder
RM		Right Midfielder
	AM	Attacking Midfielder
IL		Inside Left
	IR	Inside Right
CF		Centre Forward
	LW	Left Wing
RW		Right Wing

FW Forward

IN THE BEGINNING:
ALL-OUT ATTACK

1

THE MATCHES

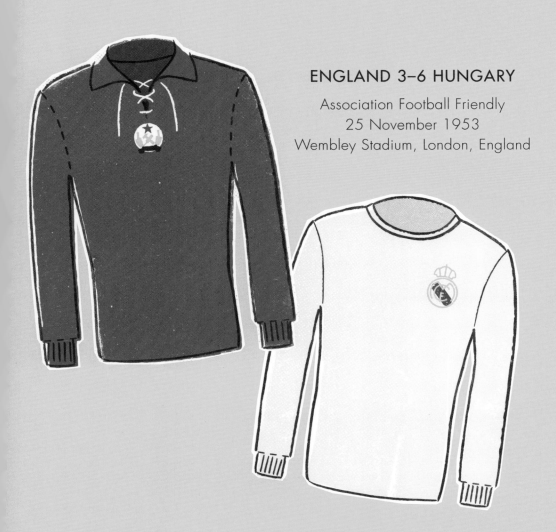

ENGLAND 3–6 HUNGARY

Association Football Friendly
25 November 1953
Wembley Stadium, London, England

REAL MADRID 7–3 EINTRACHT FRANKFURT

European Cup Final
18 May 1960
Hampden Park, Glasgow, Scotland

IN THE BEGINNING:
ALL-OUT ATTACK

The two games that feature here took place within seven years of each other. The first was a friendly and the second was a European Cup Final. Hungarian Ferenc Puskás played in both games, where his versatility was key. Both Hungary and Real Madrid exploited a more adventurous three at the back formation. The two sides also displayed more ambition in the offensive nature of their play. The positioning of their players was hard to define, in contrast to the regimented WM (3–2–2–3) formation that had dominated the game for several years.

ENGLAND 3–6 HUNGARY

ASSOCIATION FOOTBALL FRIENDLY, 25 NOVEMBER 1953
WEMBLEY STADIUM, LONDON, ATTENDANCE 105,000

So pivotal was this contest for its time – and for years to come – that it became known as the 'Match of the Century', and defined a period of change in international football. Despite a chastening experience in its first World Cup, which included a historic defeat to the United States, England remained an intimidating side to face, especially

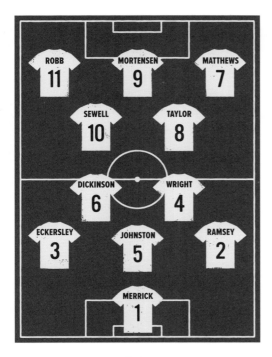

ENGLAND

GK	1	Gil Merrick
RB	2	Alf Ramsey
CB	5	Harry Johnston
LB	3	Bill Eckersley
RH	4	Billy Wright (captain)
LH	6	Jimmy Dickinson
IR	8	Ernie Taylor
IL	10	Jackie Sewell
RW	7	Stanley Matthews
CF	9	Stan Mortensen
LW	11	George Robb

Manager Walter Winterbottom

HUNGARY

GK	1	Gyula Grosics (captain)
RB	2	Jenó Buzánszky
CB	4	Gyula Lóránt
LB	3	Mihály Lantos
DM	5	József Bozsik
DM	6	József Zakariás
RW	7	László Budai
CF	9	Nándor Hidegkuti
LW	11	Zoltán Czibor
IR	8	Sándor Kocsis
IL	10	Ferenc Puskás

Manager Gusztáv Sebes

at home, where it had lost just once, four years earlier. In contrast, the Hungarian national side was seen as more progressive, having announced itself on the international scene by winning Olympic gold in 1952. The Hungarians hailed from a then communist state that invested deeply in the side. The coach, Gustáv Sebes, also happened to be the country's deputy sports minister. Their triumph at the Olympics should have alerted those involved in English football that something very special was happening in Hungary. Teams in England used the WM formation, which showcased three defenders, two sitting midfielders and five ahead of those (seen from above – as in the line-up – the positions mark the points of a W above an M). Hungary, meanwhile had begun to introduce a new concept. On the basis of its recent form, the team was the top-ranking international side in the world. It had been unbeaten for four years.

The England side featured men who would go on to become world famous: Alf Ramsey, who later managed England during their World Cup glory in 1966, and the Blackpool pair of Stanley Matthews and Stan Mortensen. This was a strong England side loaded with players of individual quality who should have been able to cope with a Hungarian team whose players were not even household names. Seven of them came from the same domestic team, Honvéd. In future years, other coaches would select as many players as possible from the same club team in order to engender a sense of continuity.

The Match

There is some debate about how many people were in attendance at Wembley that day, but there were definitely more than 100,000. It's fair to assume that the vast majority of those were English and would have been amazed by the start of the game, which saw a goal from the visitors in the opening minute. Nándor Hidegkuti was the man with that opening strike. Jackie Sewell equalised and that seemed to be a pivotal moment, with England thinking they were on the way to another easy victory. If only it could have been that easy for the hosts. Sewell would give an interview to the BBC in 2010 and had this to say about his goal:

'I nipped in between two defenders to equalise but they weren't bothered, they just carried on as they were taking us apart and thirteen minutes later we were 4–1 down.'

On the Hungarian offensive, József Bozsik played an essential role in feeding the ball through to the three players at the front.

That might well have been the best passage of football played at Wembley. Hidegkuti grabbed another on his way to a hat-trick, but perhaps the moment that lives longer in the memory came in the twenty-fourth minute when a man named Ferenc Puskás gave the

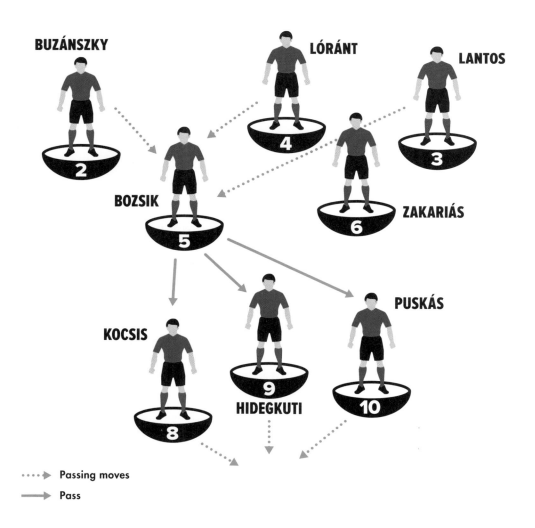

BUZÁNSZKY

LÓRÁNT

LANTOS

2

4

3

BOZSIK

ZAKARIÁS

5

6

PUSKÁS

KOCSIS

10

9

HIDEGKUTI

8

········▶ Passing moves
———▶ Pass

ATTACKING PLAY

LB

DM

GK

CB

DM

RB

Typical attacking play saw the three at the back feeding the ball down the wings to a playmaker midfield, who then fed the ball forward. For Hungary, this was Bozsik.

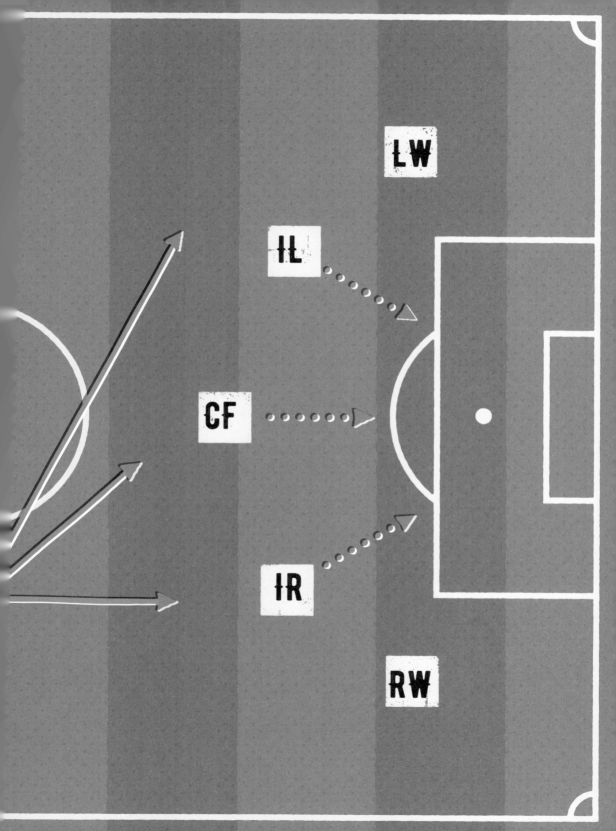

football world the 'drag back', after picking up the ball from between the right edge of the six-yard box and the penalty area. He was marked by the England captain Billy Wright and, wanting to take the ball on his favoured left foot, he performed the manoeuvre, taking it from his right side to his left and leaving Wright bamboozled, before slamming the ball into the top corner of the net.

Having been 4–2 up at half-time, Hungary added another two goals in the second half, with the last word in the scoring coming from England's Ramsey, who slotted home a penalty thirty-three minutes from time. But those watching from the stands had seen enough to give shape to their thinking.

'The game had a profound effect, not just on myself, but on all of us. That one game alone changed our thinking. We thought we would demolish this team – England at Wembley, we are the masters, they are the pupils. It was absolutely the other way,' said twenty-year-old Fulham star and future England manager, Bobby Robson, who had been in the stands. Puskás said some of his teammates thought of it as the achievement of a lifetime. They would scale more heights, reaching the World Cup Final the following year, only to lose 3–2 in the final to West Germany.

The Philosophy

Few matches in the twentieth century displayed a completely different style of football in the way this game did. It's easy to see why it is difficult to pigeonhole the formation the visitors used. The front five were notable for the use of the 'false 9' in Hidegkuti, who played in a withdrawn role, allowing the likes of more progressive players, such as Puskás, to operate in areas that suited him. The more intriguing aspect, however, was at the back. Were Hungary playing with a back three, in the same way most sides did, or were they experimenting here with a back four? Gyula Lóránt was nominally a centre back, who would sometimes work as part of a centre-back duo, but at other times as a sweeper, making sure Hungary had a player to hold his position as his colleagues rampaged up front.

To expand on both those key roles, the sweeper (Lóránt) did hold his position as the men in front of him advanced, either when in possession or to augment teammates in possession. That allowed those players almost constantly to feel as if they were in possession of the ball. If England were to advance, it would come from counter-attacks during which the opposition had overcommitted. And, usually on those occasions, England were finding themselves lacking the legs to run up and down the field, having spent much of the game chasing the ball. Hungary didn't spend time running after the ball because of the team's dominance of the game.

Lantos, Budai and Zakariás pulled back to join Lóránt when defending, and Bozsik advanced to make the most of a counter-attack.

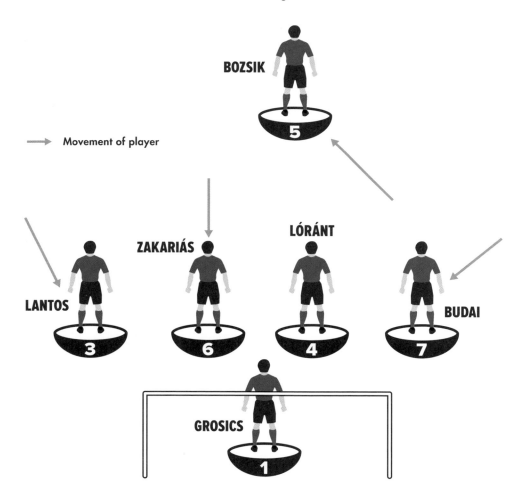

Movement of player

BOZSIK
5

ZAKARIÁS
LÓRÁNT
LANTOS
3
6
4
BUDAI
7

GROSICS
1

HUNGARY DEFENCE

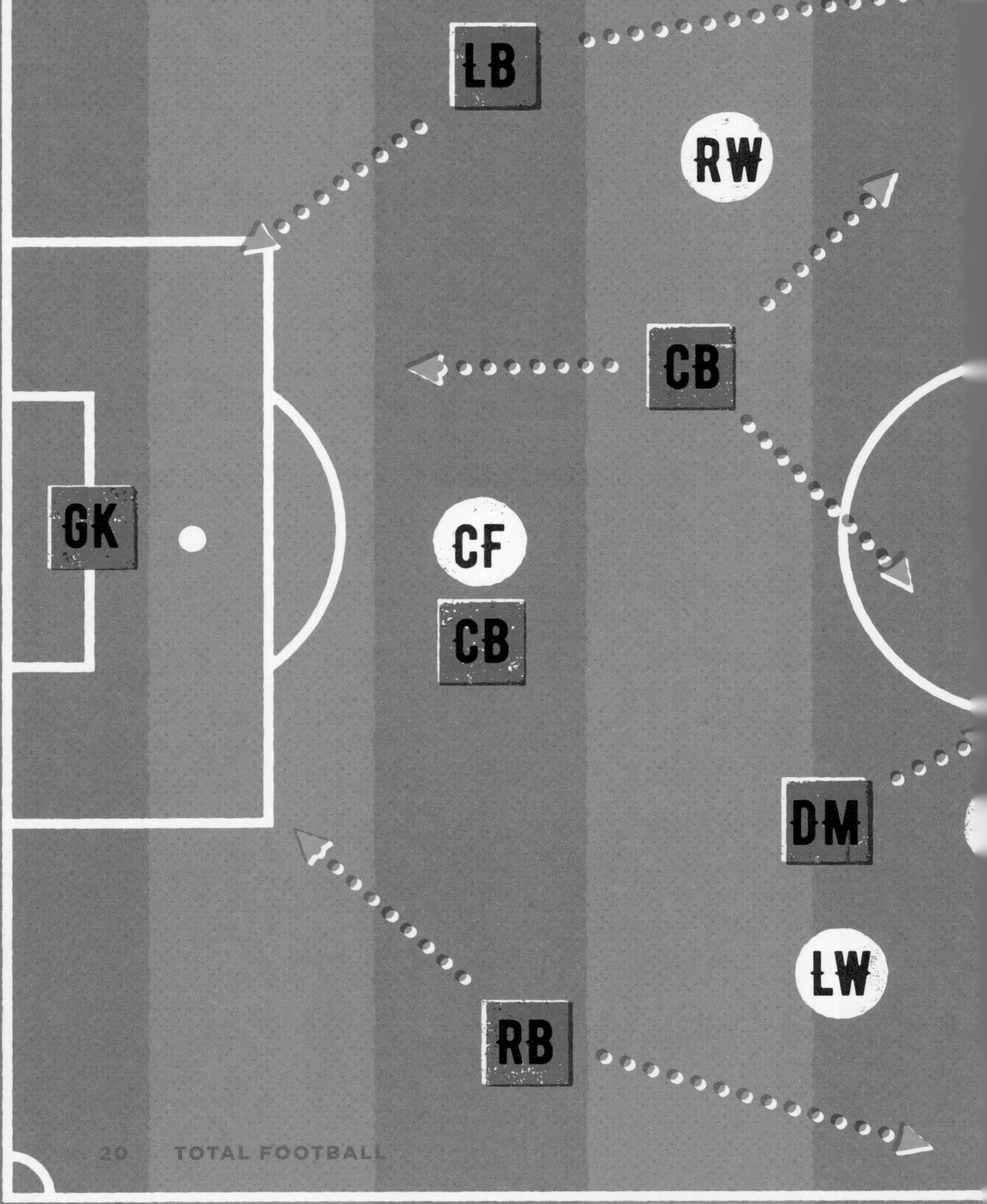

LB

RW

CB

GK

CF

CB

DM

LW

RB

Hungary

England

Range of movement

While Hungary had a starting line-up featuring three defenders at the back, the team sometimes used four men, with defensive midfielder József Zakariás dropping deeper to join Gyula Lóránt (CB), Mihály Lantos (LB) and Jéno Buzánszky (RB).

The false 9 gave the England defence a real problem. It made Hidegkuti's movement almost impossible to predict and therefore cater for. The hosts were so entrenched in their WM formation (used by England's domestic teams) that the notion that anyone else could play differently completely threw them. Puskás and Kocsis played alongside Hidegkuti and were free to move wherever they could find space. England's very traditional back three could not cope with the constant interchanging of positions. Over the ninety minutes, Hungary managed thirty-five shots on goal, compared with England's five. This game was no exception to Hungary's free-scoring ways – during a six-year period in which the 1954 World Cup Final was the team's only defeat, the players averaged more than four goals a game.

Puskás was particularly potent up front, his fluid movement around the pitch making him increasingly difficult to mark.

One other, often overlooked, tactic, saw Gyula Grosics, act as a spare defender, playing almost as a sweeper-keeper. Modern sides, particularly those managed and coached by Pep Guardiola, use the goalkeeper as an essential part of the offensive nature of the team.

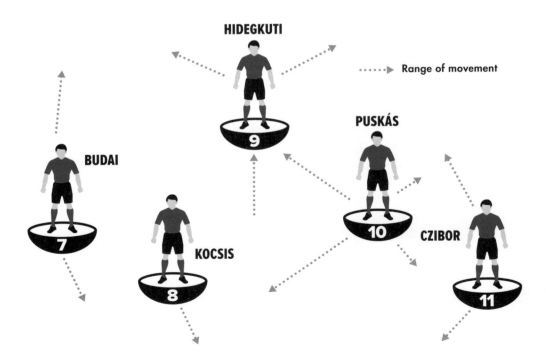

Key Player

Ferenc Puskás may well be the greatest international goal scorer ever. Despite being all left foot and slightly overweight, his ability to move to where the action was, meant that the deployment of the false 9 did not compromise his team's offensive options. His record of eighty-four goals in eighty-five games stands scrutiny with all the great players of his era. He moved effortlessly across the front three/five to give his side the fluidity that was so key to its victories. His dependence on his left foot was often called a weakness, but given what he could do with it – shoot, pass, drag back – many agreed with his assertion that 'you can only kick with one foot at a time'. He was nicknamed the 'Galloping Major' even though he rarely broke into a run. And despite his teammate Hidegkuti scoring a hat-trick that day at Wembley, few left the stadium believing they had, and would ever again, see a better player than Puskás.

Also forgotten is the influence of coach Gusztáv Sebes, who believed in a kind of football that features throughout this book. 'When we attacked, everyone attacked, and in defence it was the same. We were the prototype for total football.' These were the words of Puskás, but the thoughts came from Sebes. He believed that every man on the pitch had a role to play in the collective nature of what the Hungarians were trying to achieve. There was a socialism in his football that was married to his political aspirations. It helped him to motivate his sides when they played the likes of imperialist England. He frequently referred to socialism when he spoke to his players before the game and in any pre-match utterings to the press.

To prove that the win was no accident, Hungary would hammer England again the following year. The team would eventually be undermined by the political climate at home, with Russia's invasion in 1956 prompting many of its top players, including Puskás, to defect.

THE 'FALSE 9'

Hungary

England

Range of movement

IR

IL

Hungary exploited the 'false 9' position, where the centre forward (traditionally wearing shirt number 9) drops deep into the midfield. With Hidegkuti as the false 9, the remaining forwards had far greater freedom up front, with support from players on the wings.

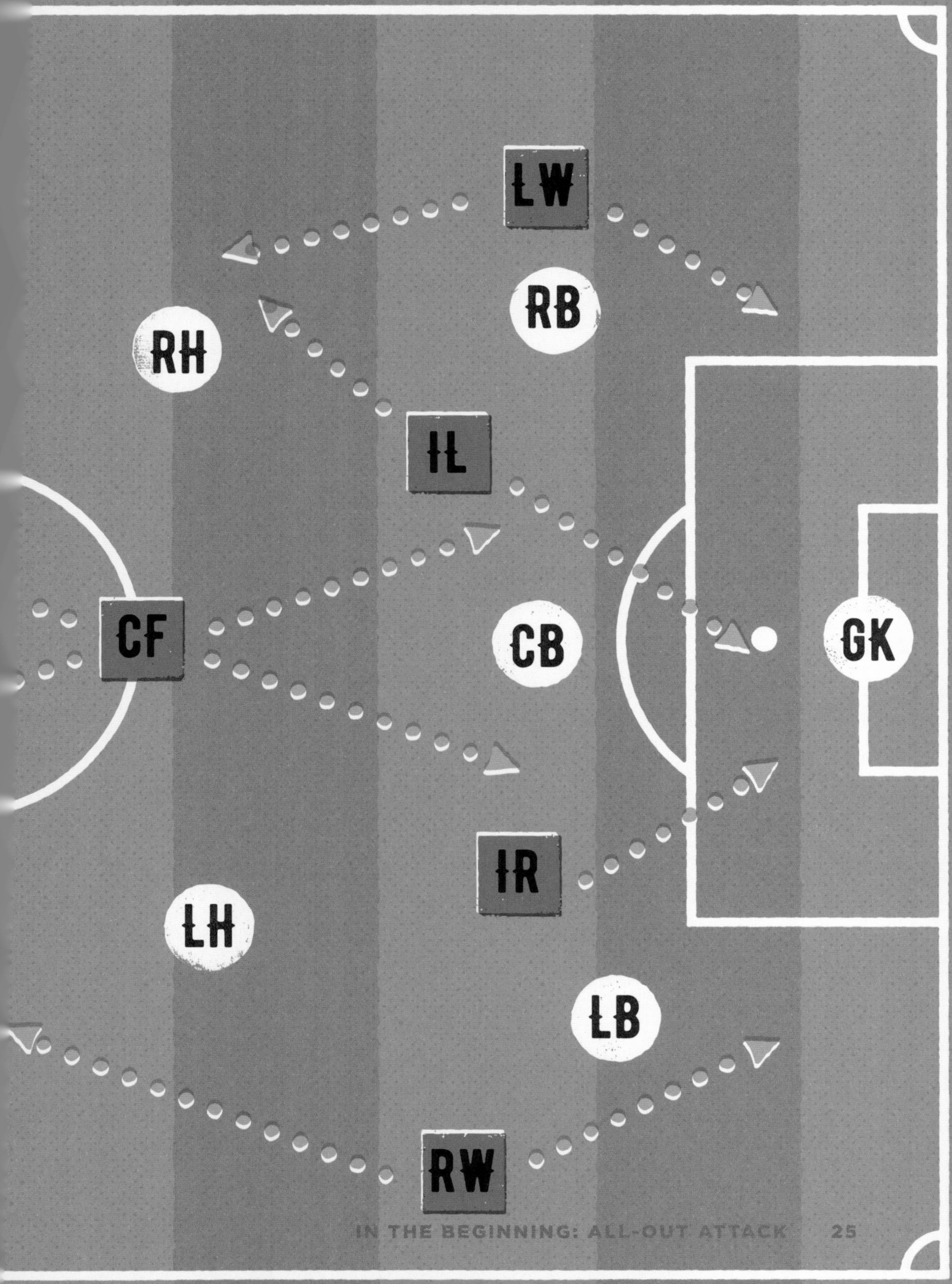
LW
RB
RH
IL
CF
CB
GK
IR
LH
LB
RW

REAL MADRID 7–3 EINTRACHT FRANKFURT

EUROPEAN CUP FINAL, 18 MAY 1960
HAMPDEN PARK, GLASGOW, ATTENDANCE 127,621

During a conversation back in 2001, the legendary Scottish sportswriter Hugh McIlvanney told me that this game *was* 'football'. He may have inserted an adjective before the noun, but I'm too much of a gentleman to disclose what it was. For many of his generation, the match will remain a standard bearer of pinnacle football for that era. Real Madrid had won the first four European Cup championships, but the fledgling competition only received the hype and coverage it deserved from a UK perspective when this final was played at Scotland's Hampden Park. The Scottish fans had been hoping to get behind Glasgow Rangers in the match, but their team had been vanquished by a free-scoring Frankfurt side in the semi-final. Given the one-sided nature of that game, many were expecting Real's crown finally to slip in this final.

Real Madrid were no longer champions of their own country – that title had been handed over to great rivals Barcelona. But it was Barca that Real had beaten in the semis on their way to Hampden Park. The team had a starting line-up that was the envy of any side: among the players were Ferenc Puskás, hero of the great Hungarian team of the 1950s, and Argentine Alfredo Di Stéfano, who was signed from South America and would score in all five of those finals. For many years, Di Stéfano was the leading Real Madrid goal scorer, ultimately overtaken by Raúl and then Cristiano Ronaldo. Alongside him and Puskás was Francisco Gento, considered one of Spain's finest ever wingers, with six European Cups and twelve league titles to his name.

Among the 127,621 people in attendance was a teenager by the name of Alex Ferguson, who left the stadium in Glasgow that evening in thrall to the immeasurable quality of the football both sides provided. In many years to come, his teams at Aberdeen and

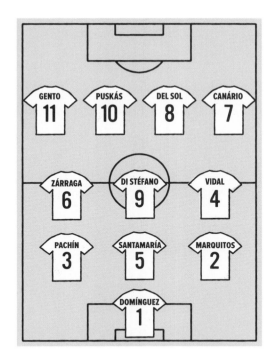

REAL MADRID

GK 1 Rogelio Domínguez
RB 2 Marquitos
LB 3 Pachín
MF 4 José María Vidal
CD 5 José Santamaría
MF 6 José María Zárraga (captain)
RW 7 Canário
FW 8 Luis del Sol
FW 9 Alfredo Di Stéfano
FW 10 Ferenc Puskás
LW 11 Francisco Gento

Manager Miguel Muñoz

EINTRACHT FRANKFURT

GK 1 Egon Loy
DF 2 Friedel Lutz
DF 3 Hermann Höfer
MF 4 Hans Wielbächer (captain)
DF 5 Hans-Walter Eigenbrodt
MF 6 Dieter Stinka
FW 7 Richard Kress
FW 8 Dieter Lindner
FW 9 Erwin Stein
FW 10 Alfred Pfaff
FW 11 Erich Meier

Manager Paul Osswald

then Manchester United would strive to deliver that same type of thrilling football, married with a basic commitment to teamwork as well as individuality. There is more on Fergie and the great United sides to come, but first stop is Hampden Park and the night that the 'Blond Arrow' wreaked havoc.

The Match

It is sometimes said in the sport of boxing that the worst thing you can do is hurt your opponent too early in the fight, thereby making him aware how dangerous you are. Eintracht Frankfurt had the temerity to score first, taking the lead in the eighteenth minute. It was the goal that woke the beast. Real scored six times before the German side found the net again. And those goals for *los Blancos* came from the boots of just two men. Di Stéfano (three) and Puskás (four) shone like beacons on an evening when their teammates were all earning their win bonuses.

But that free-scoring performance seemed a world away during the opening twenty minutes of the game, as the recently deposed Spanish champions seemed to be stuck in reverse gear. Eintracht were sharper in and out of possession and when they took the lead through Kress, a shock seemed likely. But Real would eventually respond with venom, scoring the next six goals, with three before half-time. In the second half, the Germans scored two consolation goals. But the sixth and seventh strikes from Real were the ones that would live long in the memory. Number six saw Puskás turn and swivel in the Eintracht penalty area before burying a shot high in the goal. And the seventh came straight from the kickoff, with a flowing move involving the Hungarian that took just fourteen seconds and involved five passes, all along the Scottish turf, until it was punctuated by a powerful low drive from Di Stéfano.

At 7–2, Real Madrid finally relaxed, appropriately satisfied with their efforts. One more goal from Eintracht Frankfurt made the score slightly more respectable, but did not fool anyone about the severity of the beating that had been inflicted.

The Philosophy

When a side is blessed with unique talents (Puskás and Di Stéfano), an air of pragmatism can help with its philosophy. In common with most European sides, the team utilised a back three. The coach, Miguel Muñoz, once argued that 'success is the result of discipline and big moments coming together'. But there was scant evidence of players sticking to their positions – certainly in the front seven. In contrast to Eintracht, who played quick, direct passes to their forwards, sometimes bypassing their midfield, Real were keen to

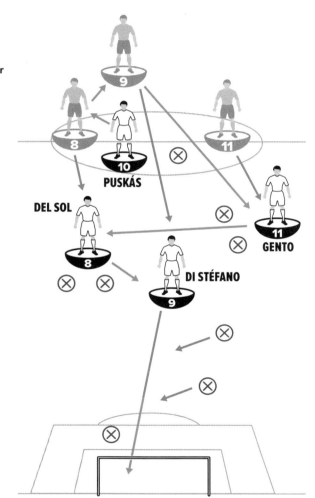

 Opposition

→ Movement of player

→ Pass

Real's seventh goal started with a Puskás pass to del Sol, who fed back to Di Stéfano. The two players then advanced, fluidly, aided by Gento.

WORKING
THE PITCH

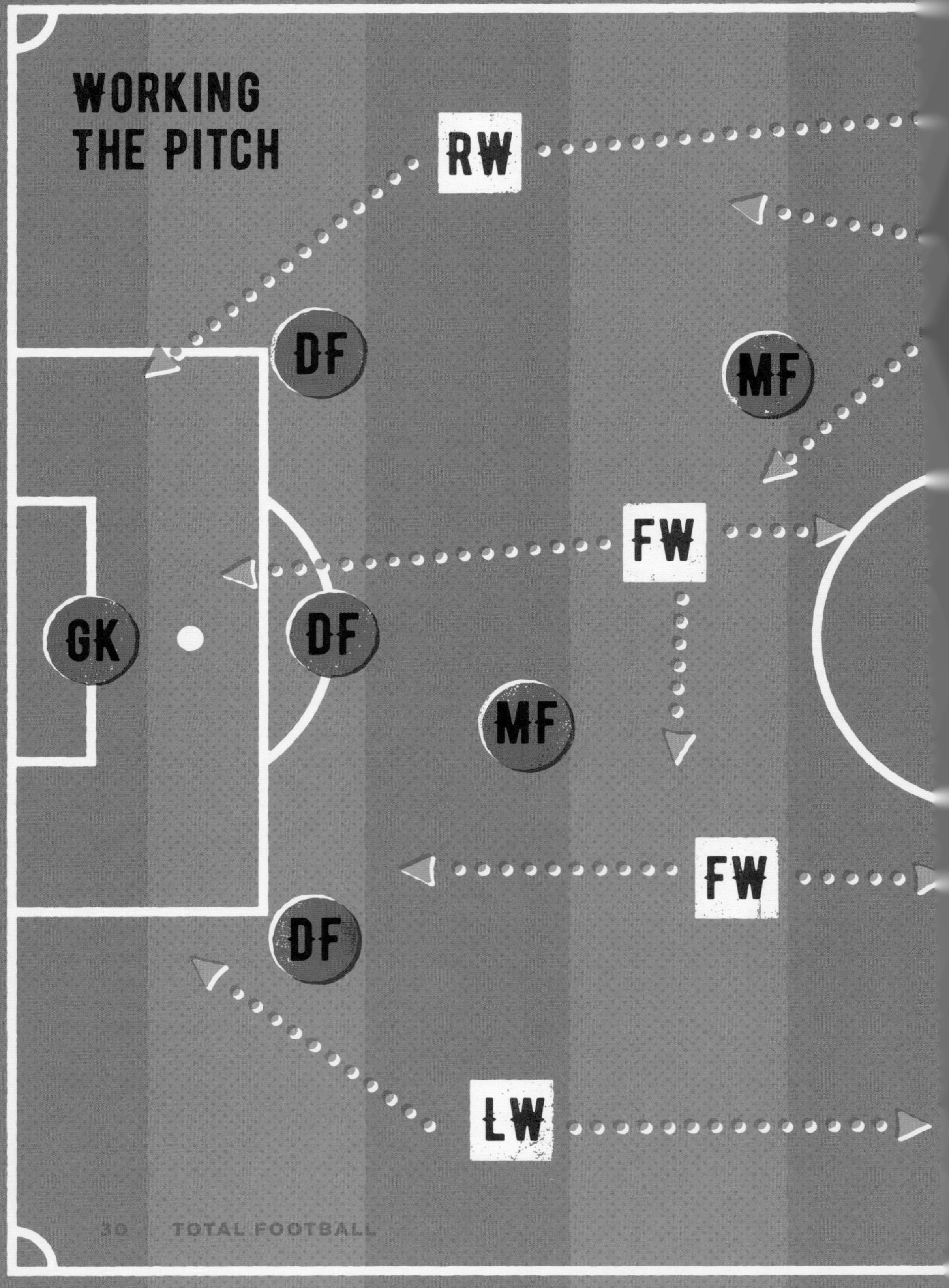

RW

DF

MF

FW

GK

DF

MF

DF

FW

LW

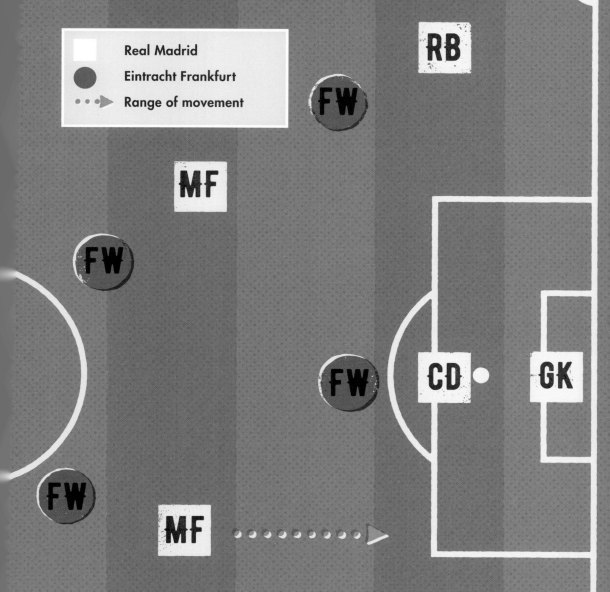

Real Madrid □

Eintracht Frankfurt ●

Range of movement •••▶

RB

FW

MF

FW

FW

CD • GK

FW

MF •••••••••▶

The Real Madrid team kept passes tight and short, working the pitch in triangular groups in order to advance. In doing so, they were able to find space more easily, so increasing the fluidity of their game.

 FW

 ŁB

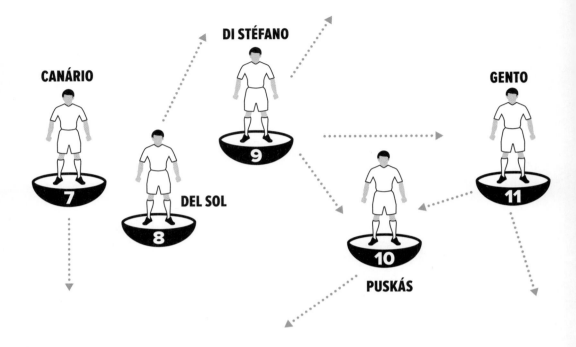

adopt a more measured set-up, with small triangles of passing designed to establish their position on the field and evade the clutches of their opponents, who were defending in the man-to-man marking system that was so prevalent in European football.

Those small triangles allowed the trio of Puskás, Gento and Di Stéfano to roam free and cause trouble. And as that trio pressed forward, so the midfield advanced, giving the opposition a feeling of being penned in. Another advantage that Real Madrid had lay in the contrast in individual ability of the team's players. While Puskás, in his mid-thirties, relied on his smarts and tactical acumen, Gento used his pace to find space for himself and other teammates.

Then there was Di Stéfano, who played in the same withdrawn striker role that we observed Nándor Hidegkuti use for Hungary against England. His movement meant that Real Madrid could sometimes advance in a five, despite lining up in a 3–3–4. This helped during those frequent passages of play when the men in white shirts were in ascendancy and gave the impression they were

Di Stéfano was key to the team's offensive strategy. Dropping back into the false 9 position, he was pivotal in keeping the ball in Real's possession.

Key Player

Even with Puskás scoring four goals, it is hard to ignore the contribution of Di Stéfano, who, instead of playing the orthodox centre-forward role, used his superior knowledge of the game to find areas of danger in which to operate. There have been many tributes to his genius, but perhaps none as adequate as that of Sir Bobby Charlton, who watched him as a spectator as an impressionable twenty-year-old.

swarming all over the pitch. In order to evade the herd of Real Madrid players, Eintracht Frankfurt frequently punted the ball upfield, surrendering possession easily. It doesn't take a rocket scientist to grasp that playing with the ball is much less tiring than chasing it for ninety minutes. The other benefit of Di Stéfano as that withdrawn striker was that he would be one of the first players to win back the ball from the opposition when counter-attacking.

'Who is this man? He takes the ball from the goalkeeper, he tells the full backs what to do; wherever he is on the field he is in position to take the ball, you can see his influence on everything that is happening . . . I had never seen such a complete footballer . . .'
Sir Bobby Charlton on Di Stéfano

Di Stéfano was an assertive player, yet he was able to put his own desires to one side for long enough to play a role as part of a team. Where there were other star players, such as Puskás, he was happy enough to share the spotlight. Perhaps the one thing that gave Di Stéfano that incredible ego was his stamina, which allowed him to keep running when others were already thinking of their post-match entertainment. If he played with a certain arrogance, he did so because he demanded from others as much as he did from himself.

HOW WE STOPPED IT: CATENACCIO

2

THE MATCH

INTER MILAN 3–1 REAL MADRID

European Cup Final
27 May 1964
Praterstadion, Vienna, Austria

HOW WE STOPPED IT: CATENACCIO

All good things must come to an end and the Real Madrid side that epitomised attacking football at Hampden Park in 1960 would not scale the same heights in a European competition again. This was partly due to age (Ferenc Puskás and Alfredo Di Stéfano were well into their thirties), but also because it is human nature to find new ways of doing things. Football was still a relatively novel pastime, and while we were slowly taking note of the greatness in Real, it was also clear that there were different ways of winning the game.

INTER MILAN 3–1 REAL MADRID

EUROPEAN CUP FINAL, 27 MAY 1964
PRATERSTADION, VIENNA, ATTENDANCE 71,333

In the 1960s, there seemed to be no obvious philosophy of football that guaranteed victory. Brazil won the 1962 World Cup and England won the trophy four years later with a team famously dubbed

INTER MILAN

GK	1	Giuliano Sarti
SW	6	Armando Picchi (captain)
RB	2	Tarcisio Burgnich
DF	5	Aristide Guarneri
LB	3	Giacinto Facchetti
DM	4	Carlo Tagnin
MF	10	Luis Suárez
MF	8	Sandro Mazzola
RW	7	Jair da Costa
FW	9	Aurelio Milani
LW	11	Mario Corso

Manager Helenio Herrera

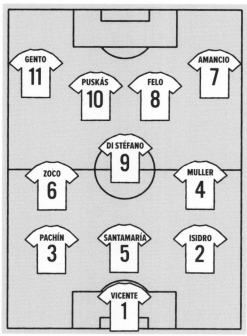

REAL MADRID

GK	1	José Vicente
RB	2	Isidro
DF	5	José Santamaría
LB	3	Pachín
MF	4	Lucien Muller
DF	6	Ignacio Zoco
FW	9	Alfredo Di Stéfano
FW	8	Felo
FW	10	Ferenc Puskás
RW	7	Amancio
LW	11	Francisco Gento (captain)

Manager Miguel Muñoz

the 'wingless wonders', yet neither side could claim that what they were practising was suddenly the vogue. In Italy, however, a new style of football was being developed, the origins of which came from Switzerland, via an Austrian coach. It was the beginning of another tactic that we have since come to know as 'catenaccio'.

The style of football associated with the tactic was new to most of the world, but came to define Italian soccer for a great many years. In terms of club football, Real Madrid proved the standard bearer for what sides wanted to achieve. The team's dazzling free-scoring, all-out-attack style was impossible to replicate without players of such quality as Puskás and Di Stéfano. But now, with Helenio Herrera as their head coach, the emerging Inter Milan side found that they were capable of scoring goals and conceding them in equal measure.

The Match

The game started with Real Madrid on the front foot, as was customary and expected. It was thought that the world's greatest strikeforce would provide a constant stream of ingenious attacking play that the Italians could not cope with. But in contrast with the click interchange of passing that fans witnessed when Real Madrid thrashed Eintracht Frankfurt in the European Cup Final of 1960, the Spanish team found a less pliable opposition in 1964. Key to this was the fact that the opposition was not accustomed to conceding goals. In winning the Italian Scudetto the previous season, Inter Milan had scored a modest fifty-four goals in thirty-four games. Of much more significance than this, was their concession of just twenty goals.

For the entirety of the opening forty-five minutes, Real found that passing lanes were not as open as they were accustomed to. Often, they would lose possession in frustration as a well-organised Inter Milan side held its position on the field. Real might well have had more of the ball, but they always seemed compromised when they did, as if the obvious pass no longer existed.

The Italian side took the lead shortly before half-time, through a rasping drive from Sandro Mazzola. He, along with playmaker Luis Suárez, was the more prominent of the Inter Milan attackers, content to work on scraps throughout that first half. Mazzola was playing as one of the midfielders, but the second goal of the game, which came sixteen minutes after half-time, was scored by the man nominally playing as a centre forward, Aurelio Milani, with a speculative shot that evaded José Vicente.

Real briefly threatened a comeback when Felo scored a spectacular goal with one-quarter of the game remaining. But a second from Mazzola, whose strong running forced a mistake from the Real defence, guaranteed that Inter Milan would win their first European Cup and keep the trophy in Milan, as their great rivals AC Milan were the reigning champions.

Man-to-man marking was key – each of the defenders had a specific member of the opposition to mark for the duration of the game.

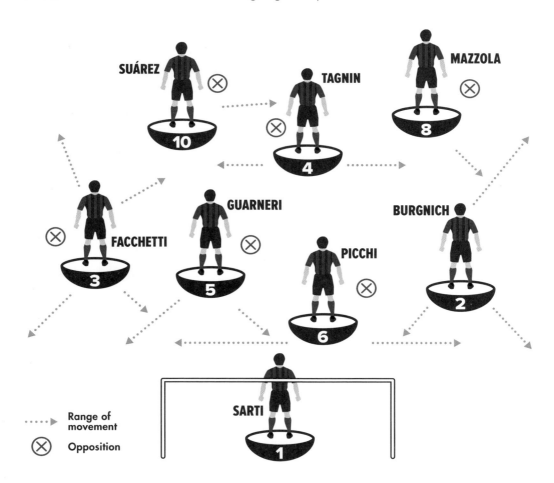

Range of movement

Opposition

TWO-LINE DEFENCE

●●●▶ **Range of movement**

LB

M

DF

GK **SW**

RB

MF

The catenaccio tactic centred on a barely penetrable defence, with the three defenders and three midfielders filling gaps to create a double bank of players, and a sweeper, or 'libero' immediately in front of the goalkeeper.

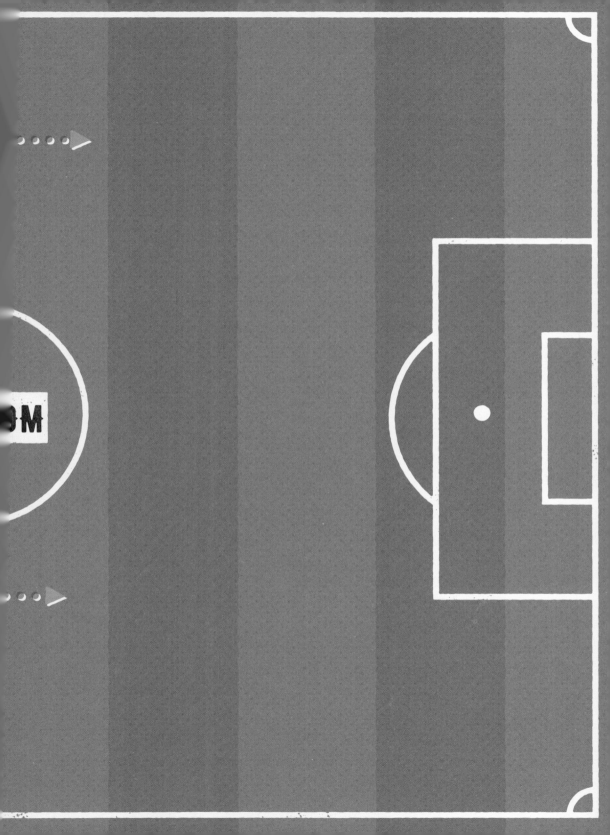

In a sad footnote, the match proved to be Di Stéfano's last for Madrid. He argued violently with manager Muñoz about the tactics used that evening and the idea that Real should have man-marked Facchetti. 'We played the game minus one player, but Muñoz told me to go to hell and they threw me out of the club because I told *him* to go to hell!', the Argentine wrote in his memoirs. It is also fair to say that Di Stéfano was a shadow of the player that had tormented Eintracht four years earlier, his thirty-eight-year-old legs no longer able to carry his body into danger areas with the same velocity and venom.

Picchi's role was to effect a swift transition from defence to attack and vice versa. Passing the ball long to Suárez, Milani or Mazzola gave others the time to make a break forwards.

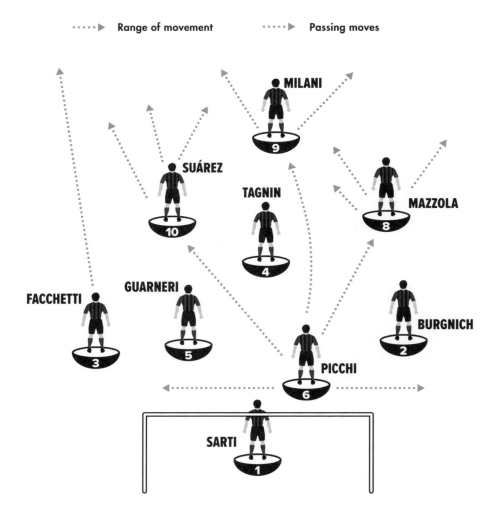

The Philosophy

The tactic 'catenaccio' has become synonymous with Italian football. The concept is probably best described by the phrase 'park the bus', used by frustrated managers whose teams fail to find a way to score against obdurate, disciplined defences. Its origins derive from Karl Rappan, an Austrian who coached the Swiss national side in the early 1930s and developed a football tactic that came to be known as the 'bolt', as an antidote to the WM system. The bolt system relied on collective, rather than individual talent, with each of the players given a specific role as part of defensive, midfield and attacking units. The main innovation was to play one defender as a spare man behind the back three. Essentially, this meant that sides using the bolt system would line up in a 1–3–3–3 formation. Rappan used the tactic for his Swiss side, enabling them to beat superior opposition at the 1938 World Cup.

Herrera developed the system further at Inter Milan. The primary enhancement was the use of that spare defender as a 'libero', or sweeper. His role not only involved stopping any attacks that evaded the back three, but also instigating a return offensive. It was the offensive development of the position that gave rise to the term 'libero', which means 'free' in Italian. Future liberos would include the likes of Ruud Krol, Matthias Sammer and the legendary Franz Beckenbauer – three players adept at ending opposition attacks and then starting one of their team's own. In the fullness of time, the role of the libero has been absorbed into that of a centre back. But in the 1960s, this tactical innovation allowed teams such as Inter Milan to compete internationally with those of superior firepower. Throughout this final, Real enjoyed plenty of possession, but when they had the ball, Inter formed a protective base designed to shield their four-man defence, and were ready to spring forward on regaining the ball.

As if to demonstrate this, when Inter Milan scored the opener, only three of the team's players were in their own half. The goal came from a shot outside the penalty area from Mazzola, but there were four Inter Milan players within passing range for the midfielder. In modern football, we associate 'park the bus' football with long balls

THE 'LIBERO'

●●●▶	**Range of movement**
●●●▶	**Passing moves**

LB

SW

M

The libero instigates the counter-attack, sweeping up the ball and playing it long to one of the team's midfielders, who then drives it forwards, sometimes pushing it out to the wings.

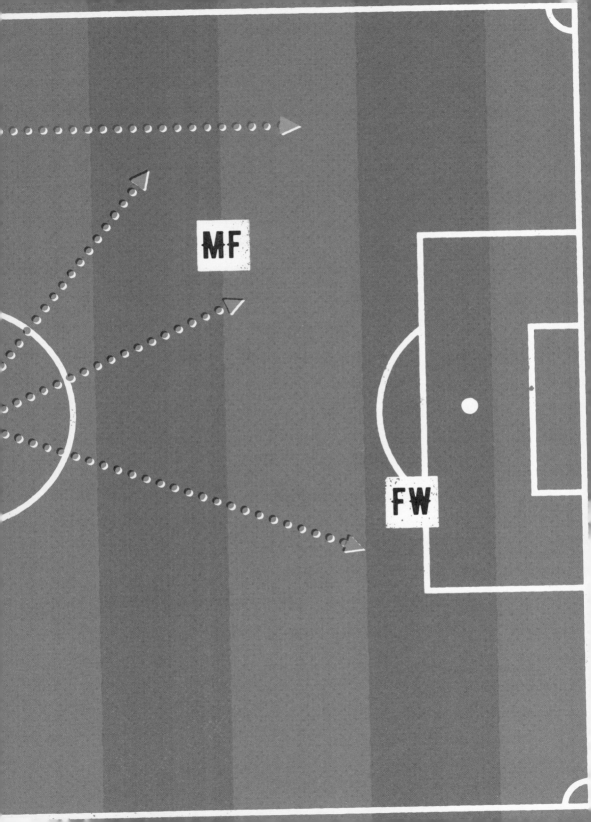

Key Player

While many great liberos were tall or fast, Armando Picchi was neither. At just 174 cm, Picchi was considerably shorter than his fellow defenders and the opposing attackers. But he was the epitome of a man who knew his role within the side and did not seek anything other than to help his team. His coach, Herrera, began to implement the catenaccio style in 1962 and Picchi was a vital cog in his Inter Milan machine, eventually becoming captain. He may have had more talented teammates, such as Giacinto Facchetti, but he was expert at allowing those ahead of him to take possession of the ball and orchestrate attacks. With Picchi as a sweeper, Inter Milan won three Serie A titles, two European Cups and two Intercontinental Cups. His greatest achievement was to convince the national side of his worth in the 1966 World Cup. Prior to that, it was felt he was too defensively minded to be effective on the world stage.

played to large, physical strikers or a reliance on set pieces to score the majority of the goals. But this Inter Milan side, at its peak, knew when and how to attack and when to defend. And now that Real's top players were past their peak, so too was the team. In contrast to the way Inter Milan were playing now, this Real side had relied on the talents of its players rather than philosophy.

The philosophy of the football played by Inter Milan was defined by the idea that a side could not lose if it did not concede a goal. Certainly this was the case if it did not concede the first goal. By scoring first, Inter Milan could press home their advantage by then seeking to make sure that Real could not advance with any freedom. The double bank of defence in front of the sweeper made it hard for Real to make any inroads.

The problem with catenaccio came when everyone started to use it in Italy, resulting in games devoid of entertainment. It's a great way to stop sides that play expansive, attractive football, but as the sport evolved, and with the introduction of three points for a win in

Inter's third goal came from Mazzola pressing the Real Madrid defence and forcing an error.

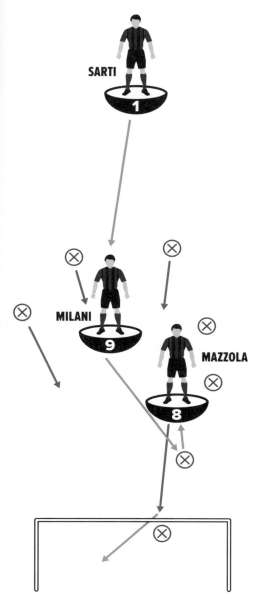

leagues, the strategy got left behind – in order to win, teams almost inevitably had to be more of an attacking side and it was no longer enough simply to rely on not conceding a goal. The tactic's decline was precipitated by the 1970 World Cup and the 'total football' played by the great Dutch sides of the early 1970s, which introduced the idea of playing offside as a form of defence, which is harder to do with a libero in operation.

Though the tactic declined, it has not died altogether – it still represents an almost guaranteed way of preventing goals being conceded and therefore winning at least one point. Versions of the tactic have been seen as recently as the 2004 European Championship, when Greece emerged victorious after scoring early and then defending for the remainder of a match. A modern take on the tactic is to deploy the spare man between the defence and midfield, as seen when Italian Antonio Conte's Chelsea beat Tottenham Hotspur at Wembley in 2017. José Mourinho is also associated with catenaccio-style football. His version of the tactic was much more progressive and could be witnessed in his Inter Milan side that won three trophies in 2010, and subsequently, his Chelsea team of 2013/14, which was able to beat Manchester City and Liverpool, free-scoring teams that proved unable to manage a goal against Chelsea at their own stadiums.

→ Movement of player

→ Pass

⊗ Opposition

3

BRINGING BACK THE LIGHT

THE USE OF THE NUMBER 10

THE MATCH

BRAZIL 4–1 ITALY

World Cup Final
21 June 1970
Estadio Azteca, Mexico City, Mexico

BRINGING BACK THE LIGHT

THE USE OF THE NUMBER 10

Any conversation about football between people of a certain age will likely include a summation of the 1970 World Cup and '*that* Brazil team'. It is easy to forget that Brazil were in a state of disarray going into this tournament. The gold and green had won the World Cup in 1958 and 1962, but the previous tournament, held in England, proved to be something of a watershed. Just months before the 1970 tournament began, Brazil opted to change their coach and bring in Mário Zagallo, who had played in the winning 1958 side.

BRAZIL 4–1 ITALY

WORLD CUP FINAL, 21 JUNE 1970
ESTADIO AZTECA, MEXICO CITY, ATTENDANCE 107,412

The catenaccio style of football detailed in the previous chapter was becoming less and less attractive. The 1970 World Cup, played in high-altitude Mexico City, featured glorious attacking play, defined by a few matches: namely, Brazil's defeat of cup holders England in the group stages, the holders' eventual elimination at the hands of

BRAZIL

GK	1	Félix
DF	4	Carlos Alberto (captain)
DF	2	Brito
DF	3	Piazza
DF	16	Everaldo
MF	5	Clodoaldo
MF	8	Gérson
FW	7	Jairzinho
FW	9	Tostão
FW	10	Pelé
FW	11	Rivelino

Manager Mário Zagallo

ITALY

GK	1	Enrico Albertosi
DF	2	Tarcisio Burgnich
DF	8	Roberto Rosato
DF	5	Pierluigi Cera
DF	3	Giacinto Facchetti (captain)
MF	10	Mario Bertini
MF	16	Giancarlo de Sisti
MF	13	Angelo Domenghini
FW	15	Sandro Mazzola
FW	20	Roberto Boninsegna
FW	11	Luigi Riva

Manager Ferruccio Valcareggi

former West Germany in the quarter-finals and then Italy's ascent to the final with a 4–3 victory over the Germans in the semi-finals.

But it was the Brazil team that won all the plaudits, following a string of victories. In the five games leading up to the final, they had scored a total of fifteen goals, with Jairzinho scoring in every game. The team had conceded five as well, and it was no secret that, as good as the players were going forward, they could also be vulnerable at the back. But, overall, the team was much improved on that of previous years, having learned lessons from their campaigns. According to Gérson, the team had learned from its European counterparts: 'We knew how to play, they knew how to run.'

The Match

With the match underway, two key elements were clear from the start. Firstly, that playing football at altitude immediately reduces the pace of play. Secondly, this game was a brutal one; tackles were robust from players on both sides, and frequently cynical. With Pelé busy considering a permanent international retirement, he tackled as hard as he was being tackled himself. Misplaced passes and wasted set pieces were the common theme for the first seventeen minutes. But then Brazil took the lead when Rivelino, who had wasted opportunities so far, crossed for Pelé to leap and head the ball into the net. Italy had threatened from the beginning of the match and equalised when Brazil over-played in defence and Boninsegna rolled the ball past the already advanced Félix.

The following half an hour (either side of the half-time whistle) saw this Brazil side grow tenser and tenser. For all the kind words that had been written about this team, the players were all too aware of the fact that winners receive much more in the way of plaudits. It was in the sixty-sixth minute that Gérson, so often the fulcrum of the side, took the ball from thirty yards out and hit it with the kind of swerve that seemed to be easily imparted in the altitude of Mexico City.

Within five minutes, Jairzinho had scored his customary goal, before a piece of football genius that has lived long in the memory. Playmaker Tostão won the ball back for Brazil in his own half and a triangle of passes ensued before Clodoaldo's mazy dribble took away three tiring defenders. His lay off to Rivelino saw the winger drill a pass to the feet of Jairzinho, who cut inside and passed to Pelé. The world's greatest player was twenty yards from the goal and could have shot. But sensing something more special was about to happen, he simply rolled the ball to his right, into space. That spot of unfettered grass was soon occupied by a sprinting Carlos Alberto, the right back and captain. His first-time shot buried itself into the far corner of

Brazil's fourth goal: Jairzinho's cross-field run with the ball gave Alberto time to make the run down the right wing, and score.

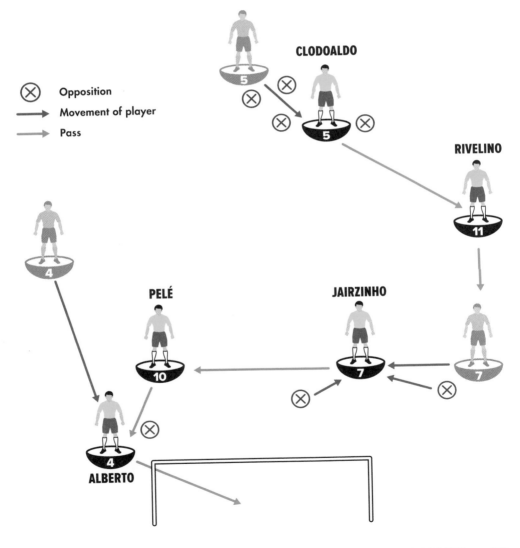

CLODOALDO

RIVELINO

Opposition

Movement of player

Pass

PELÉ

JAIRZINHO

ALBERTO

ALBERTO'S GOAL

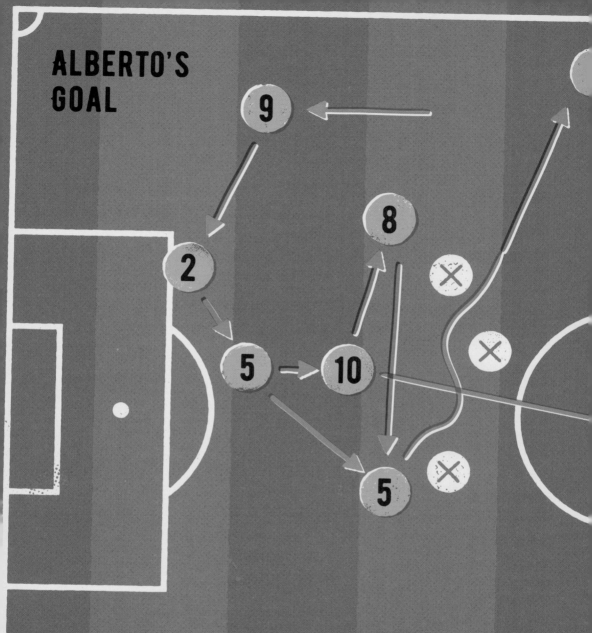

Possibly the most talked about goal in the history of the World Cup, Brazil's fourth goal came just three minutes before the final whistle. The action starts with number 9, Tostão, making a pass to number 2, Brito.

	Brazil
	Opposition
→	Movement of player
→	Pass

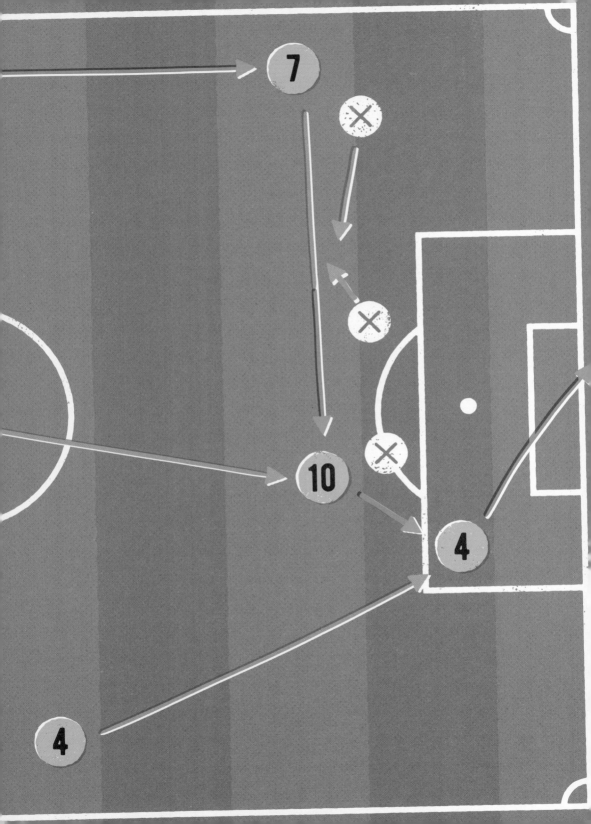

the goal. As an expression of something wonderful and unique, it is beyond compare in World Cup finals. It is perhaps beyond compare in any other kind of football tournament.

The Philosophy

There are so many aspects to Brazil's triumph that require further investigation. Perhaps the first is the proliferation of players with similar qualities. Zagallo picked a 4–2–4 formation, but it has been argued frequently that the front six were all players who operated best as a number '10'. Nominally, the two were Gérson and Clodoaldo and in front of them were Rivelino, Pelé, Tostão and Jairzinho. But it was impossible to say that this was a rigid 4–2–4 formation. All players switched effortlessly and when they did for the fourth goal, the results were sublime.

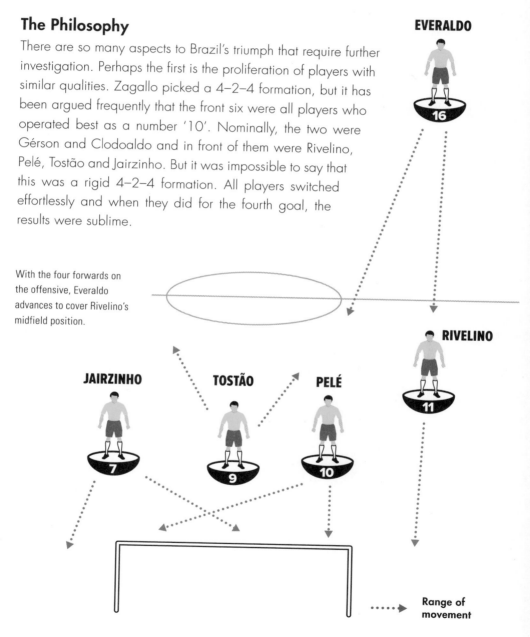

With the four forwards on the offensive, Everaldo advances to cover Rivelino's midfield position.

Range of movement

In that goal, Jairzinho, who was playing off the right, picked up a long ball from Rivelino who had swapped left wing for left back. Pelé went central after forward partner Tostão had gone back into his own half to reclaim the ball and start the move. And it was Carlos Alberto, marauding from right back, who applied the finishing touch.

There are many sceptics who say that coach Zagallo did not have a philosophy aside from picking his best players and hoping that it worked. But in picking Clodoaldo, who was essentially an 'enforcer' type midfielder, and giving Gérson responsibility for acting as the deep lying playmaker, shedding his more attacking instincts, there was definitely a method. This, too, could be seen as an expression of total football, when players could swap positions for the common goal. Short passing and ease of movement were the order of the day and so the abundance of players who played in similar roles aided this team in its freedom of movement.

It is said that this team had no defence and an eccentric and unreliable goalkeeper. And yet Félix made a crucial save from Italy in the first five minutes and the team kept the defending champions at bay. Perhaps the real secret to this Brazil side's success was that its true formation on the field was difficult for all to identify with, apart from the coach and players.

'Because we played as a block, compact . . . leaving only Tostão up field. Jairzinho, Pelé, Rivelino all tracked back to join Gérson and Clodoaldo in the midfield. I'm happy to see the team in terms of 4–5–1. We brought our team back behind the line of the ball. We didn't want to give space for the Europeans to hit us with quick counter-attacks. Our team was not characterised by strong marking. Our method of defending was to position ourselves in zones, cover the space and not carry out man-to-man marking. If we had gone with high-pressure marking then by the second half we would have run out of gas. So we saved our energy, dropped back, and then when we won possession the technical quality of our team stood out.' *Zagallo in conversation with South American football journalist, Tim Vickery, 2011.*

FORWARD INTERCHANGE

● ● ● ▶ **Range of movement**

GK

●

MF

Zagallo's Brazil lined up with a 4–2–4 formation, but it was clear from the start that there was far great fluidity among the players. The four at the front continually exchanged places in order to find space.

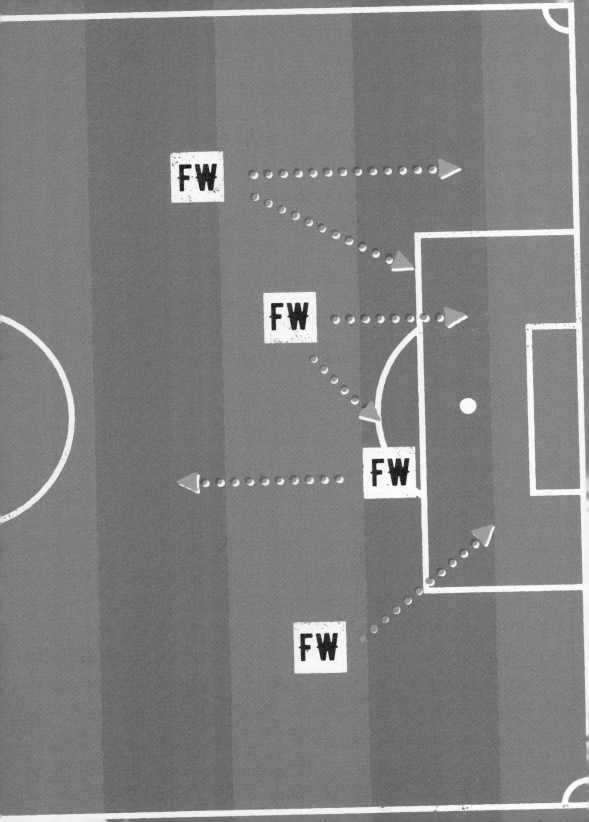

Zagallo confided in Vickery that his side had trained at altitude for three weeks to get the players' bodies conditioned to the factors that would face them during the tournament. The coach's great talent, apart from selecting a formation that could draw an opposition onto them, was also his man-management. Pelé had not seen eye-to-eye with the previous coach, João Saldanha – it was common knowledge that Saldanha thought the star was going blind. Zagallo embraced Pelé and built a team around him. And he also made sure that Gérson understood how important his role was as playmaker. He took a gamble on Rivelino, who was perhaps not the player that Paulo César was. But the latter was not on form, whereas Rivelino's dribbling could be key. Zagallo's gamble paid off. Rivelino established himself as a part of three successive Brazil World Cup campaigns.

Perhaps the secret of Zagallo's team was that so many players had an effect that it was hard to work out who the most dangerous player was. In a way, it was total football, with men interchanging positions freely and defying categorisation. Another way to assess Brazil's play, is to compare them with Pep Guardiola's 2016–17 Manchester City team. The Spaniard's side operated with one holding midfielder (Fernandinho) and then a front five, with four players who operated as number 10s and a striker. When it seems as if all of a team's best

For Jairzinho's goal, he and Pelé effectively swapped sides, with Tostão holding the centre midfield. The move caught out Italy's defence.

players are operating regardless of their formation, it's a headache for the opposition. As Italy learned in 1970, even the strongest defence can be outsmarted when competing against a team that has a deep-lying midfielder of Gérson's calibre directing the offensive. Chelsea, English Premier League champions in 2017, found that they could not keep Manchester City at bay in the 2017–18 season, with City's Kevin De Bruyne playing a role similar to Gérson some forty-seven years earlier – perhaps proof that football philosophies live long after their teams have fulfilled their destiny.

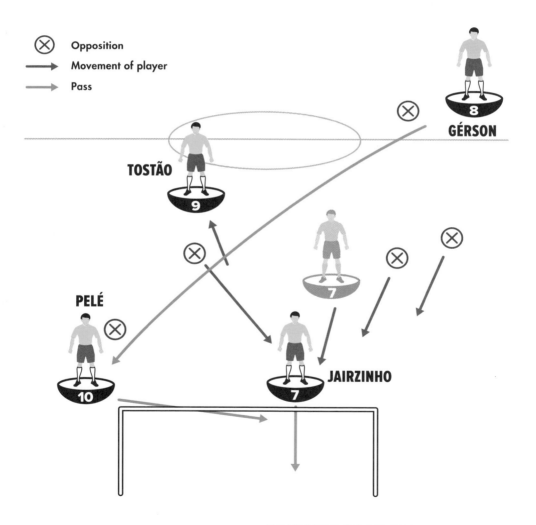

Opposition

Movement of player

Pass

GÉRSON
8

TOSTÃO
9

PELÉ
10

JAIRZINHO
7

7

TOTAL
FOOTBALL

4

THE MATCHES

AJAX AMSTERDAM 2–0 INTER MILAN

European Cup Final
31 May 1972,
De Kuip, Rotterdam,
Netherlands

NETHERLANDS 2–0 BRAZIL

World Cup
3 July 1974
Westfalenstadion, Dortmund, West Germany

TOTAL
FOOTBALL

In the mid-1960s, a man called Rinus Michels took over as manager at Ajax Amsterdam, where he set about instilling a new philosophy of 'total' football that has since had a huge influence on many other ways of playing the game. In order to bring in such a new way of playing, one needs to be a pretty good teacher; you can tell someone to do something once, but in order for that person to do it constantly, they must be taught.

Michels had been a key player for Ajax Amsterdam during the 1940s and 1950s, and returned with the Dutch national league still in its infancy. His coaching career had started at semi-professional level, while working as a gymnastics teacher. He had also worked a great deal during the 1950s under the Englishman Jack Reynolds, whose football ideals are generally regarded as the founding moments of total football. (Reynolds worked with Vic Buckingham, a former Tottenham Hotspur player, who shared similar views on how football should be played.)

In 1965, Michels took the reins as Ajax head coach, with perhaps the minimum requirement being that he made them perennial contenders for the Dutch Eredivisie – the equivalent of the Premier League in the UK. The revolution taking hold in Dutch football first became apparent in 1966, when Ajax defeated Bill Shankly's Liverpool in the European Cup. The first leg, held in the Netherlands, ended 5–1 in favour of the Dutch. The second leg ended 2–2, meaning that Liverpool suffered their record aggregate defeat in

Europe. Just one year earlier, the team had reached the semi-finals of the competition and was regarded as a European powerhouse; now it had lost to a team with little international profile. The result proved that, despite England being world champions at the time, a patient passing style, akin to that which made Hungary and Real Madrid so successful in the 1950s, was still at the forefront of the most effective ways of playing the game.

One of the key factors in making the system work even better for Ajax Amsterdam was a young man named Johan Cruyff, who had scored three of the seven goals in the tie against Liverpool that year. Nominally, Cruyff was a centre forward, but in this new dynamic brand of football, he could play in virtually any position on the pitch – apart from in goal, perhaps.

Ajax's moment did not come that season. It didn't come in the 1968–69 season either, when the team reached the final for the first time, only to suffer a heavy defeat to AC Milan. But this was all part of an upward journey, as Michels subtly tinkered with his side over the years. Ajax were the dominant team in their own country between 1966 and 1970, but the side's finest moment came in 1971, when it won the first of three consecutive European Cups. The team retained the cup a year later and aimed for a third consecutive victory when facing Inter Milan in Rotterdam, in 1972.

AJAX AMSTERDAM

GK	1	Heinz Stuy
DM	3	Wim Suurbier
DF	13	Barry Hulshoff
DF	12	Horst Blankenburg
DF	5	Ruud Krol
MF	15	Arie Haan
MF	7	Johan Neeskens
MF	9	Gerrie Mühren
FW	8	Sjaak Swart
FW	14	Johan Cruyff
FW	11	Piet Keizer (captain)

Manager Stefan Kovacs

INTER MILAN

GK	1	Ivano Bordon
DF	2	Mauro Bellugi
DF	6	Tarcisio Burgnich
DF	5	Mario Giubertoni
DF	3	Giacinto Facchetti
MF	4	Gabriele Oriali
MF	8	Gianfranco Bedin
FW	7	Jair da Costa
MF	10	Sandro Mazzola (captain)
MF	11	Mario Frustalupi
FW	9	Roberto Boninsegna

Manager Giovanni Invernizzi

AJAX AMSTERDAM 2–0 INTER MILAN

EUROPEAN CUP FINAL, 31 MAY 1972
DE KUIP, ROTTERDAM, ATTENDANCE 61,354

By the time this match was taking place, Stefan Kovacs was managing Ajax Amsterdam, Michels having left to manage Barcelona. The team contained ten Dutchmen and one German, while the Inter Milan side had ten Italians and a lone Brazilian. Three members of the Italian starting line-up had been on the pitch when Inter Milan won their first European Cup in 1964. Eight years earlier, the club had won the first of its trophies, with a side built on rigid defensive structures. Now the team was playing a side that used its attacks as the best form of defence. Both sides went into the match with a back four, but while Inter Milan started with two holding midfielders, and three ahead of them, with Roberto Boninsegna playing as a lone striker, Ajax played a much more fluid 4–3–3.

The Match

The set-ups of the two teams led to much of the first forty-five minutes being played in the Inter Milan half. Johan Cruyff – operating as a centre forward, but with licence to roam free – was often at the start and end of moves. Midway through the first half, seven Inter Milan players were seen defending in their own penalty area, their offensive players relying on clearances rather than penetrating passes and therefore on the fringes of the game. Ajax got the ball in the net midway through the half, with what looked like a header from Cruyff, but that actually ended up in the net via his outstretched arm.

Inter Milan also started the second half having to defend. Ajax broke up a tired-looking Inter attack just six yards outside the Italian side's area and a cross to the far post was missed by keeper Ivano Bordon, only to be stroked into an empty net by Cruyff.

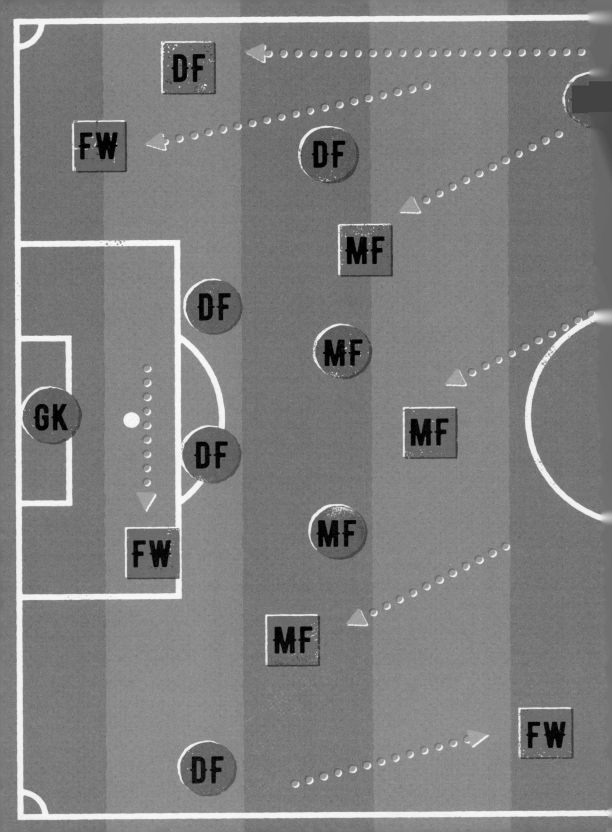

PRESSING PLAY

	Ajax Amsterdam
	Inter Milan
• • • ▶	Range of movement

Ajax Amsterdam spent much of the game against Inter Milan pressing on the attack. Effectively, this forced the game into the Inter half of the pitch, with the Italians having to defend heavily.

That was in the forty-seventh minute. Shortly after, a foul took place in the Inter penalty area and was adjudged as obstruction. In modern football, a penalty would have been awarded; here, Ajax gained an indirect free kick, but failed to make anything of it. They extended their lead nevertheless, in the seventy-sixth minute of the game, with a powerful header from Cruyff. Inbetween the two goals, Inter Milan increased their attacks slightly but still didn't commit to an offensive approach: two wide players joined the centre forward, with the midfield players ten yards further upfield. Still, Ajax controlled the bulk of play and looked more dangerous. The superior fitness of the Dutch players and ill-judged game management of the Italians (for example, players committing fouls to break up attacks) helped the Dutch team to its second European Cup victory.

THE NETHERLANDS 2–0 BRAZIL

WORLD CUP, 3 JULY 1974
WESTFALENSTADION, DORTMUND, ATTENDANCE 53,700

While the Ajax players were making a lot of football dreams reality, the Dutch national side seemed to be on the verge of its own kind of history. The team had recruited Rinus Michels as its head coach for the 1974 World Cup. Despite their impressive record at these championships in the latter part of the twentieth century, the Netherlands did not have a rich history at the World Cup to date.

But there was a sense that the 1974 tournament would be different. Dutch clubs had won the European Cup from 1970 through to 1973. And in Johan Cruyff, the country had the world's best player. Cruyff's relationship with coach Michels was special, in that both men trusted each other within the confines of their player/ coach relationship.

Michels was obviously the coach, but Cruyff was very much his leader and orchestrator on the pitch. The Dutch campaign in 1974

THE NETHERLANDS

GK	8	Jan Jongbloed
DF	17	Wim Rijsbergen
DF	12	Ruud Krol
DF	20	Wim Suurbier
MF	3	Willem van Hanegem
MF	2	Arie Haan
MF	13	Johan Neeskens
MF	6	Wim Jansen
FW	16	Johnny Rep
FW	14	Johan Cruyff (captain)
FW	15	Rob Rensenbrink

Manager Rinus Michels

BRAZIL

GK	1	Émerson Leão
CB	3	Marinho Peres (captain)
CB	2	Luís Pereira
RB	4	Zé Maria
LB	6	Marinho Chagas
DM	17	Carpegiani
DM	11	Paulo César
AM	21	Dirceu
RW	7	Jairzinho
DM	13	Valdomiro
LW	10	Rivelino

Manager Mário Zagallo

THE OFFSIDE TRAP

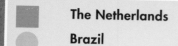

■	The Netherlands
●	Brazil
→	Movement of player
→	Pass

Unable to match the Brazilian players with their superior technical skill, the Dutch team caught the South Americans out time and time again using the offside trap.

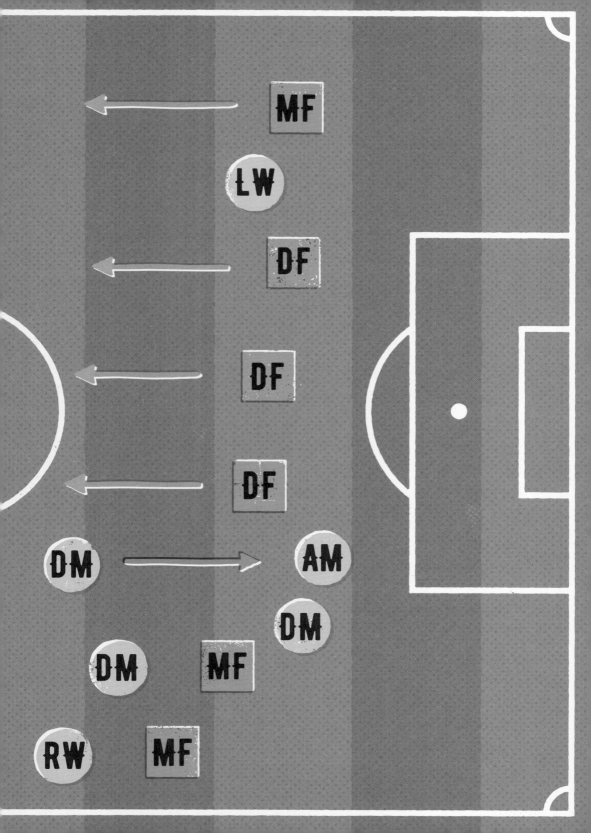

was impressive. In the five games prior to this one, they had scored twelve goals and had only conceded one, and that was in a 4–1 victory over Bulgaria.

As opposed to the current format of the tournament, which goes into a knockout stage following the initial group stages, in 1974, the teams went on to a further group stage. In this, the Netherlands beat Argentina 4–0 and former East Germany 2–0. That meant their final game against Brazil was essentially a semi-final. Both sides had won their two matches in Group A, with Brazil coming through a bruising contest against fierce rivals Argentina.

The weight of history was not on the side of the Netherlands; Brazil were three-time winners of the title and defending champions. This was only Holland's third World Cup, having appeared at the 1934 and 1938 editions. Brazil might not have had Pelé any more, but there were still players of the stature of Jairzinho and Rivelino, as well as Mário Zagallo as their coach. The one thing that would give the Netherlands real hope, was that the champions had struggled for goals: they had drawn blanks in both their opening matches.

The Match

Dortmund, in former West Germany, was the venue for this contest, which was billed as the irresistible force against the immovable object. The re-telling of this match has changed much since it took place, but it must be acknowledged that it was a very physical contest with numerous uncompromising challenges. Brazil fielded a back four, while the Netherlands started with a back three, although the shape of the side varied depending on the state of play and the whims of the players. One of the key elements of the Netherlands side was the team's ability to keep a defensive line so rigid that it could play the offside trap without much difficulty.

The great Brazil side of 1970 was known for hitting the sides from all angles, and being particularly dangerous midfield. Runners came from deep in the pitch, therefore evading the attentions of their diligent manmarkers. The team failed to make such dents this time, however, perhaps because its players were not as good as previous years, but also because the opposition had found a convincing method for stopping the Brazilian style of play. Such defending required a lot of trust and understanding from the Dutch teammates.

Despite this being a Brazil side that lacked the dynamic thrust of 1970, the team still competed on an even basis during the first half of the match. But the closest either side came to scoring during those forty-five minutes was when Cruyff had a left-footed shot saved.

Given his pre-eminence in world football, it was only natural that Cruyff would be involved when the deadlock was broken. Five minutes into the second half of the game, Cruyff combined with Johan Neeskens to score the team's first goal. Neeskens won a header that released Cruyff down the right. He then moved centre to half-volley a cross from Neeskens past the outstretched hand of Brazil keeper Emerson Leão. Within fifteen minutes, the Netherlands had doubled their lead, working a crossing opportunity down the left, which Cruyff poked into the net with a volley from close range.

During the match against Brazil, the Netherlands goalkeeper also took on the role of sweeper.

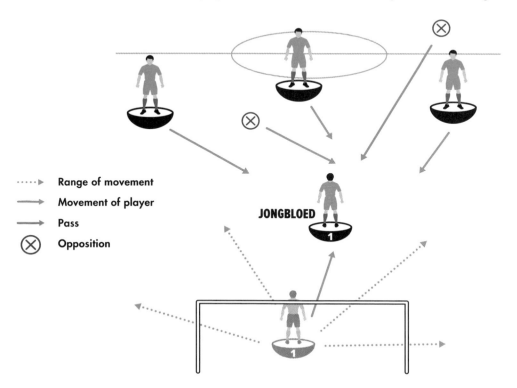

Range of movement

Movement of player

Pass

Opposition

JONGBLOED

The Brazilians suffered one final indignation. The team's central defender, Luís Pereira, was sent off in the final six minutes of the game for a scything foul on Neeskens. In truth, any one of three or four players could have seen red on the day. Despite such an impressive victory and performances during the tournament, the Netherlands went on to lose the final to West Germany, despite taking the lead. The country that gave – and still gives – so much to world football has not won a World Cup championship, having suffered two final defeats since.

The Netherlands versus Brazil. No sooner did a Brazilian player gain possession of the ball, all Dutch players in proximity closed in on him.

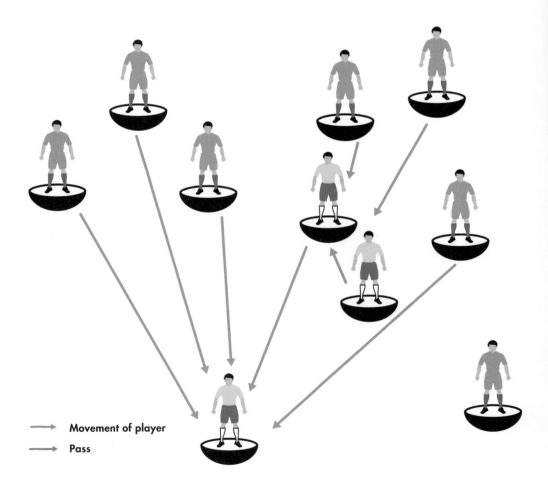

Movement of player

Pass

The Philosophy

More than forty years have elapsed since the world was exposed to total football and its influence can still be felt. Even if it had foundations in England, it was the Dutch who ultimately developed the philosophy. At the root of it was the idea that every player should be capable of being more than his position on the team-sheet. Cruyff may have been thought of as a striker, but he was capable of playing in several different positions. In the Netherlands' first goal against Brazil, his involvement started on the right wing and Neeskens – nominally an attacking midfielder – came into the centre to convert as a conventional centre forward.

The ability of players to move into different positions may seem obvious now because all the best teams follow that pattern, but in the early 1970s, it flew in the face of generally perceived wisdom. The WM formation was a thing of the past, but the majority of teams hadn't settled on a flat back four and variations of a 4–3–3 or 4–4–2 formation. In club football, Ajax Amsterdam favoured a 4–3–3, but with a degree of fluidity. The 4–3–3 formation could easily go to three at the back with a sweeper stopping any speedy counter-attacks. But the other principle to aid their attacking was for any player (aside from the keeper) to cover for someone who decides to attack. And that could be any player.

What also can't be underestimated was the influence of Rinus Michels on the players – he didn't just have a philosophy, he also primed his players fitness and tactical discipline and made sure the work was done before a game so that the final message to his players was simple:

'You never went on the field weighed down by what you had to do. [Michels] recognised your ability and he gave you some respect that in the heat of the game you would do the right thing. He didn't give you a plan that had to be slavishly followed. He said we were good enough players to understand what was required.' *Ruud Krol*

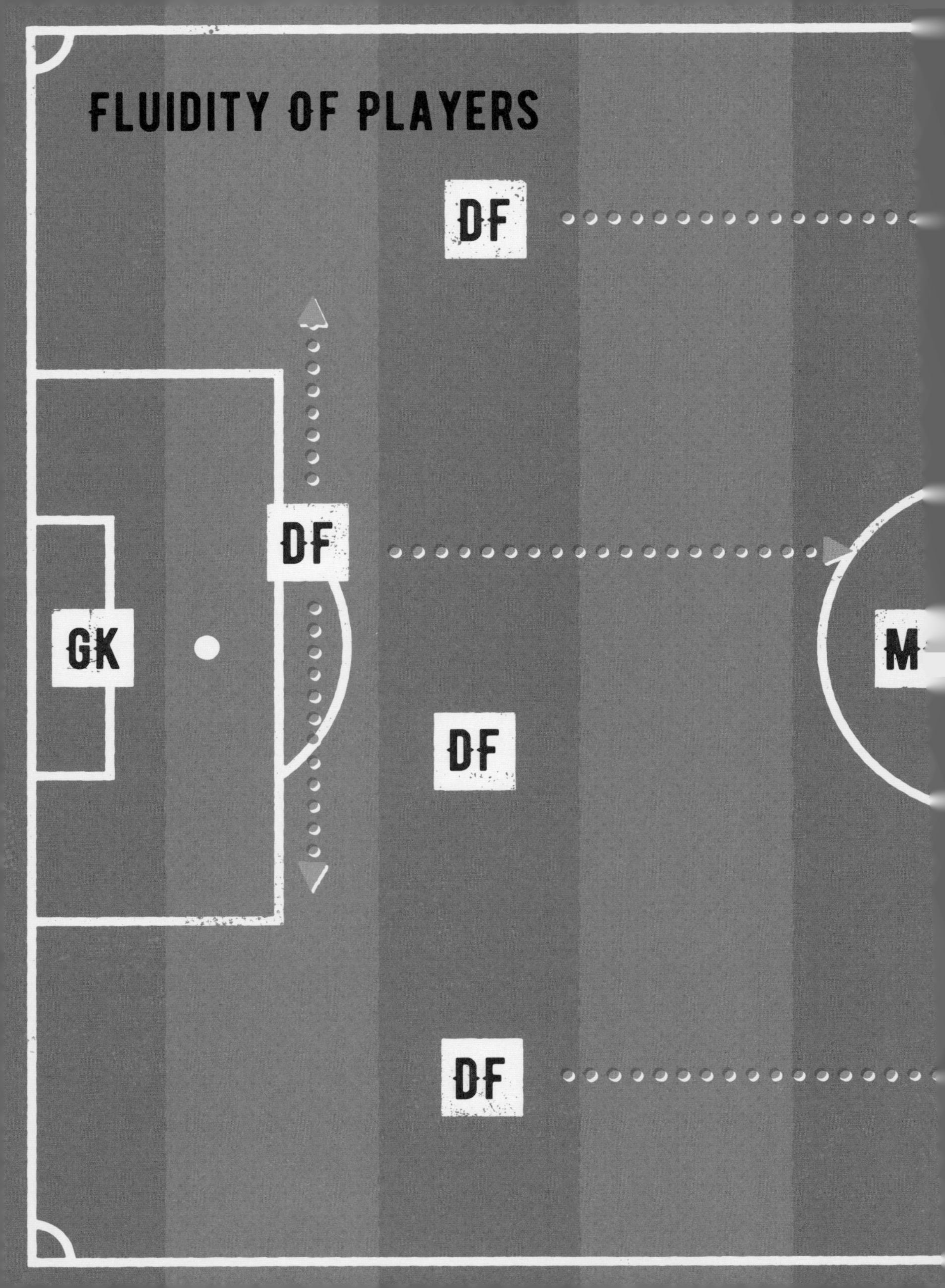

FLUIDITY OF PLAYERS

DF

DF

GK

DF

DF

M

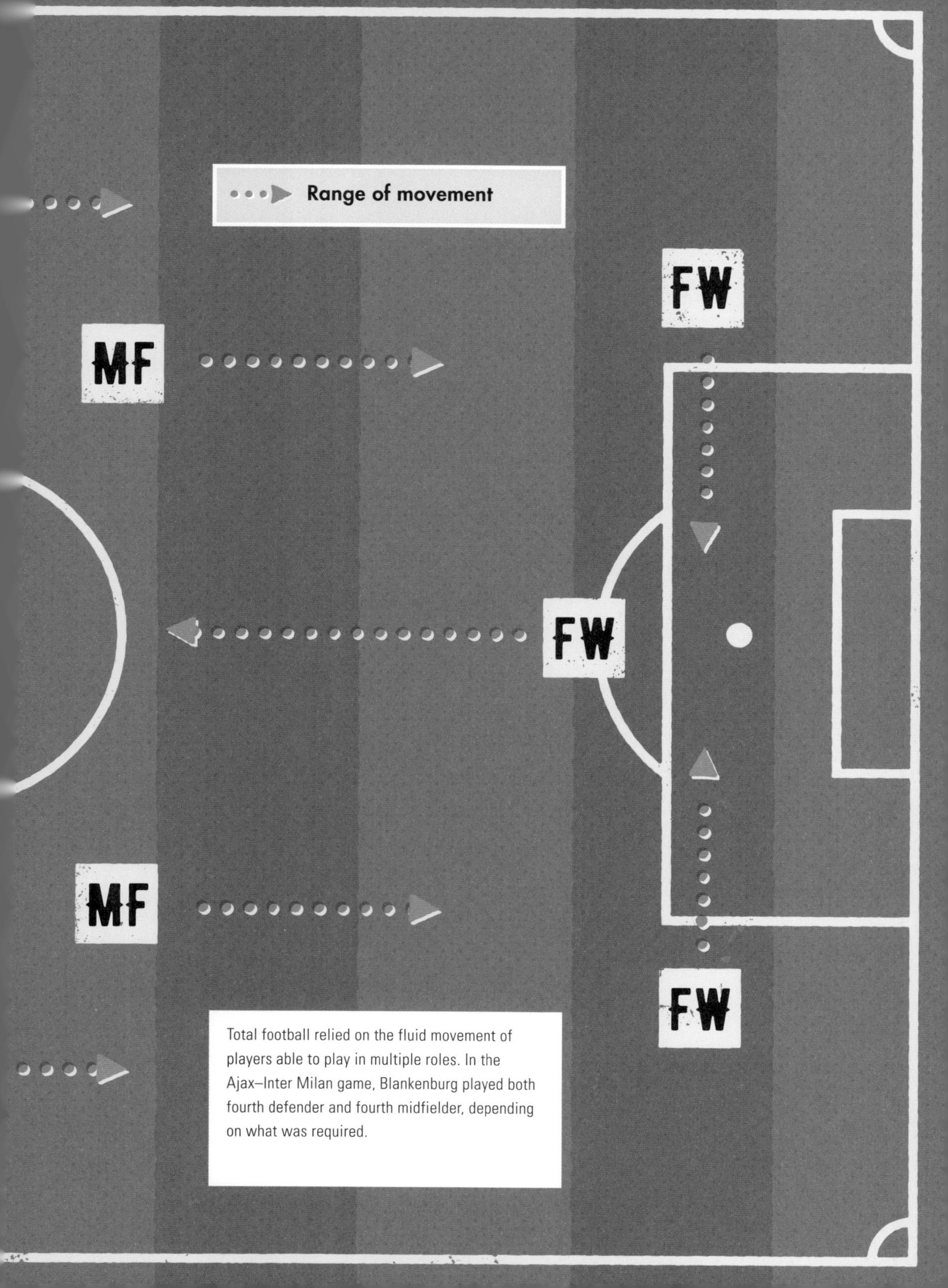

Range of movement

MF

FW

FW

FW

MF

Total football relied on the fluid movement of players able to play in multiple roles. In the Ajax–Inter Milan game, Blankenburg played both fourth defender and fourth midfielder, depending on what was required.

In order to facilitate that free movement of players all over the pitch, the Dutch (whether the national team or Ajax Amsterdam) played a high defensive line. For that to work, the whole team had to press the opposition when it had the ball. In modern terms, Jürgen Klopp, who has managed Mainz, Borussia Dortmund and took over at Liverpool in 2015, is regarded as a manager who likes his team to press all over the field. He usually instructs one of his players to lead or 'trigger' the press. For the Dutch in 1974, it was Neeskens who combined a goal threat with a tenacious workrate.

From an attacking point of view, total football sought to make the pitch as large as possible through the use of wide players, be they defenders, midfielders or forwards. Another of Michels' innovations was to invite his goalkeeper to take a more advanced role. The use of a goalkeeper as a sweeper meant that Michels could ask one of his defenders to take greater risks in his attacking play, secure in the knowledge that his duties were now being fulfilled by another person who would not be asking to swap positions with him.

Michels was able to make all these innovations because he had an assistant manager on the pitch in Cruyff. 'He had the same ideas about football', says Dutch football journalist, Tom van Hulsen. 'They trusted each other. He knew Cruyff could tell his teammates how to deal with certain situations. When you find two people that have similar thoughts then something special can happen. Of course, it helped a lot that Cruyff was one of the best players in the world.'

They needed little luck – there were some truly great Dutch players available to Michels, irrespective of his total football philosophy. The likes of Krol, Johnny Rep and Arie Haan were all-time great players, and their greatness meant they could adapt to the system. Also key were the midfielders of Neeskens and Wim Jansen, whose hard work in retrieving the ball meant the system always worked with the utmost fluidity. If the image of the Dutch players of this era is perhaps undermined by the knowledge that Cruyff managed to maintain his fitness despite a heavy dependence on cigarettes, read this from Ajax winger Piet Kiezer on the fitness regime that Michels imposed on the squad:

Typical Ajax play on the defensive against Inter Milan: defenders formed a solid back line, while Neeskens closed down on the man with the ball.

'His was the hardest physical preparation I ever had. We sometimes had four sessions a day. He also introduced the Italian system of taking players away for a period of concentrated training before a big match. We would start work in the morning and carry on until the evening . . . he was very strict with the players and there were lots of arguments about discipline. The message was pretty clear; those who did not like it would have to leave.'

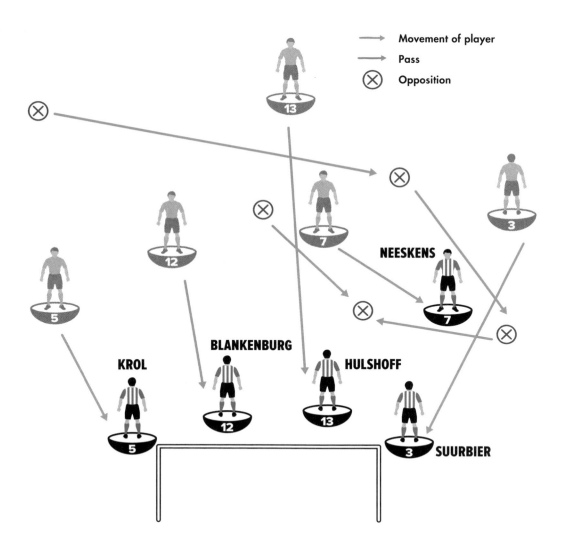

Movement of player

Pass

⊗ Opposition

NEESKENS

BLANKENBURG

KROL HULSHOFF

SUURBIER

Much of the success of total football came down to the fact that the players could change position in a linear movement, always maintaing shape, with a clear diamond in the midfield.

STUY
1

····▶ **Range of movement**

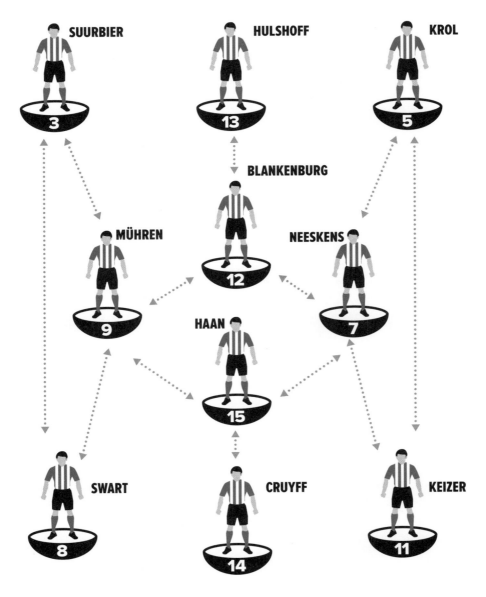

SUURBIER
3

HULSHOFF
13

KROL
5

BLANKENBURG

MÜHREN
9

12

NEESKENS
7

HAAN
15

SWART
8

CRUYFF
14

KEIZER
11

Key Player

Johan Cruyff was regarded as the most influential player of his generation and the two matches in this chapter demonstrate why. Aside from the immense skill he brought to the two teams – and his goals – it was his ability to act as his coach's eyes on the pitch that set him apart from other players of his era. The total football system relied on many things, but high on the list was trust. Michels knew that beneath the number 14 shirt beat the heart of a man with an idealistic approach to the game of football that just happened to be similar to his own.

Although West Germany's tactic of man-to-man marking and flooding the midfield prevented glory in 1974, Michels was able to inspire another generation of Dutch players in 1988 when they won their only major international trophy, the European Championship. It was that same style of football that so inspired Barcelona, managed by Cruyff in the 1980s and 1990s. There is no doubt that the style also had an effect on a young Spanish man named Pep Guardiola learning his way in football as a player under Cruyff, who then went on to manage Barcelona in 2008, Bayern Munich in 2013 and, from 2016, Manchester City.

5

MADE IN ENGLAND

(WITH A LITTLE HELP FROM THE SCOTS)

THE MATCH

LIVERPOOL 3–1 BORUSSIA MÖNCHENGLADBACH

European Cup Final
25 May 1977
Stadio Olimpico, Rome, Italy

MADE IN ENGLAND
(WITH A LITTLE HELP FROM THE SCOTS)

Despite their wealth of involvement in football, and the money spent nationwide on the game, England had contributed very little to the sport in terms of trophies. The 1966 World Cup and a European Cup two years later (both of them won on home soil) made for a distinctly underwhelming contribution. Such great sides as Manchester United and Leeds United may have dominated the English league for many years, but they had made little impact in mainland Europe.

LIVERPOOL 3–1 BORUSSIA MÖNCHENGLADBACH

EUROPEAN CUP FINAL, 25 MAY 1977
STADIO OLIMPICO, ROME, ATTENDANCE 52,078

A quiet revolution was gathering momentum at Liverpool. The team had gone from being a mid-table, second-division side at the end of the 1950s to a perennial contender in the top division by the 1970s.

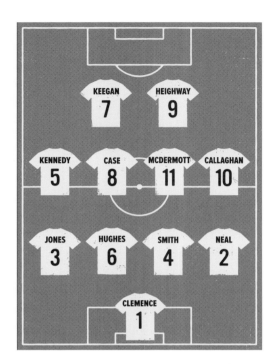

LIVERPOOL

GK	1	Ray Clemence
RB	2	Phil Neal
CB	4	Tommy Smith
CB	6	Emlyn Hughes (captain)
LB	3	Joey Jones
RM	10	Ian Callaghan
CM	11	Terry McDermott
CM	8	Jimmy Case
LM	5	Ray Kennedy
CF	9	Steve Heighway
CF	7	Kevin Keegan

Manager Bob Paisley

BORUSSIA MÖNCHENGLADBACH

GK	1	Wolfgang Kneib
RB	5	Rainer Bonhof
CB	4	Hans-Jürgen Wittkamp
CB	2	Berti Vogts (captain)
LB	3	Hans Klinkhammer
DM	10	Frank Schäffer
CM	9	Uli Stielike
CM	6	Horst Wohlers
CF	7	Allan Simonsen
CF	11	Josef Heynckes
LM	8	Herbert Wimmer

Manager Udo Lattek

More interesting, was the fact that they didn't seem to play football in the same way that other English clubs did. Having been transformed under the leadership of Bill Shankly, Liverpool had won three league titles, two domestic cups and the European Cup during his fifteen years as manager. When the charismatic Scot shockingly resigned in 1974, and his assistant Bob Paisley took over, the club barely missed a beat. The side won back-to-back league titles and another European Cup in Paisley's first three years in charge.

The year, 1977, was shaping up to be one of Liverpool's finest ever. Having already won the domestic league, the team stood on the verge of a unique treble, with an FA Cup Final against historic rivals Manchester United, followed by the European Cup Final against German side, Borussia Mönchengladbach, just four days later in Rome. But Liverpool were flat at Wembley for the first final, with manager Paisley later admitting that he had picked the wrong formation. On that occasion, he had favoured a 4–3–3 formation, which went against his preferred 4–4–2. For the next game, he restored Ian Callaghan, the team's most experienced player, in place of centre forward David Johnson.

The European Cup Final was to be the last game in a Liverpool shirt for Kevin Keegan, who was about to leave for Hamburg in the former West German league. Smaller than the average striker, he was regarded as one of the hardest-working players of the era and his endless running promised to make it a long night for Borussia and their skipper Berti Vogts, who had been so instrumental in West Germany winning the World Cup three years earlier. Vogts was detailed to do a man-marking job on Keegan in this game. His side featured just one non-West German player, the Dane Allan Simonsen, while nine of Liverpool's starting eleven were from England.

The Match

Both teams were playing in their first European Cup Final and both used a flat back four. Whereas Liverpool had reverted to their favoured 4–4–2, the German side was playing a 4–3–3. One of the most obvious deviations of this was the use of Vogts, who was a centre back, to track Keegan's every movement. Vogts's instructions seemed to mirror those of his teammates, who spent most of the first half engaged in rearguard action. It was during a brief excursion into Liverpool territory that the opening goal for the English side came about. The recalled Ian Callaghan won the ball in central midfield and then fed Steve Heighway who was, like Keegan, playing as a roving striker. Heighway moved infield and slid a pass to Terry McDermott, a midfielder who frequently broke through the line. So good was Heighway's pass, that McDermott finished without even checking where the goalkeeper was.

Much of Liverpool's play was based on short passes from one player to the next, with an emphasis on players working in triangles.

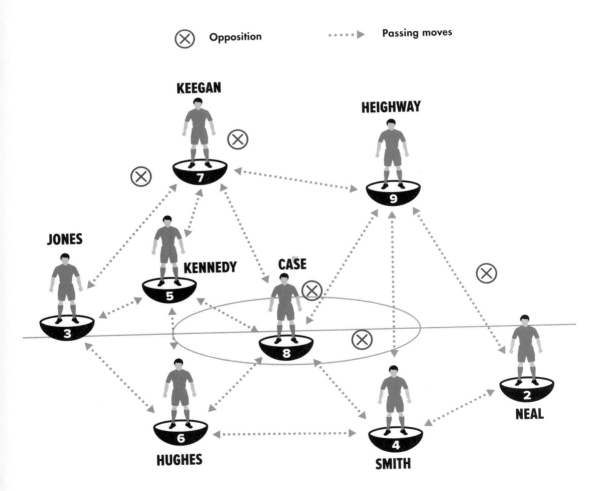

Opposition   Passing moves

KEEGAN

HEIGHWAY

JONES

KENNEDY   CASE

HUGHES   SMITH

NEAL

MIDFIELD DOMINATION

LB

CF

CM

CB

CF

CB

LM

With their preferred 4–4–2 formation, Liverpool were able to dominate the midfield with a good number of players who were equally flexible in their range of movement.

RB

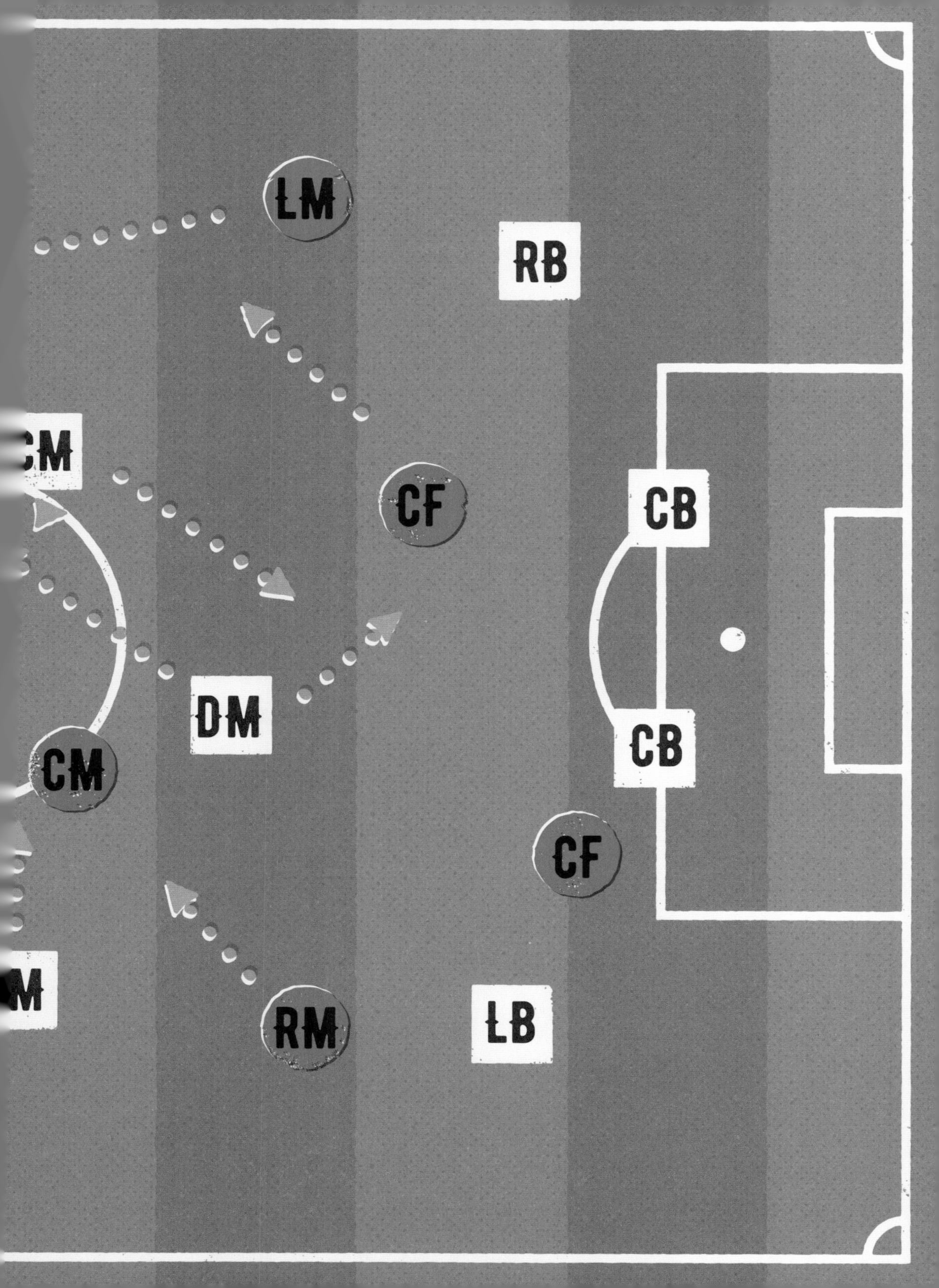
LM
RB
CM
CF
CB
DM
CB
CM
CF
M
RM
LB

Liverpool continued to be in the ascendancy until seven minutes into the second half, when Allan Simonsen capitalised on a loose pass made by the Liverpool defence and lashed a left-footed shot into the net. This prompted the best moments of Borussia's game. They nearly took the lead, but were denied by the reflexes of goalkeeper Ray Clemence, who was off his line, thwarting Josef 'Jupp' Heynckes.

In the sixty-fourth minute, Liverpool regained the lead – veteran defender Tommy Smith thumped a corner in from the left, taken by Heighway. The Reds still had to be watchful though, as Simonsen, who was the reigning European footballer of the year, nearly equalised again. In the final seven minutes of normal time, Keegan picked up the ball ten yards from the halfway line and dribbled towards the Borussia goal until Vogts brought him down for a penalty that was converted by Phil Neal.

Liverpool managed to play out until full time for their first European Cup. In the spirit of the 1970s, the team retained the trophy the following season, as had first-time winners Ajax Amsterdam and Bayern Munich earlier in the decade. For Liverpool, the triumph in

Pressing the opposition was key to Liverpool's maintaining possession for much of the game. Players closed down on whoever had the ball.

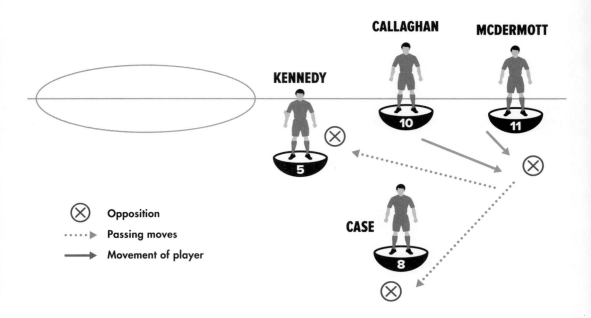

CALLAGHAN MCDERMOTT

KENNEDY

⊗ Opposition

·····▶ Passing moves

——▶ Movement of player

CASE

Rome represented the first of four wins in seven years. Only Neal survived in the starting line-up for all of those triumphs, but the team remained the most dominant side in England, as well as in Europe.

The Philosophy

Two managers had built the Liverpool side that won in Rome. Before Paisley, Shankly had put plans in place for Liverpool to be a 'bastion of invincibility', as he called it. That never happened, but he did oversee a revolution at Anfield. Rather than focus on tactics in the way that other managers did, the bulk of Shankly's training consisted of small five-a-side matches. There was also an emphasis on honing technical and preparation work, and on getting adequate rest.

This system of how to work became known as the 'Liverpool Way' and it continued well into the 1980s. That it remained intact for so long owed much to Shankly's assistants, some of whom succeeded him. Paisley, his right-hand man for many years, took over in 1974, and when Paisley retired, Joe Fagan took his place. Those three, along with others, such as Ronnie Moran, Roy Evans and Reuben Bennett, made up the famed bootroom, in which plans for games were formalised and current and future players discussed. No doubt, it was in that inner sanctum that the men exchanged views about the ways in which other teams played the game. Although Shankly put a brave face on a heavy defeat to Ajax Amsterdam in 1966, he also discovered how his team could improve in mainland Europe.

The five-a-side games enhanced his key beliefs on the pitch, which were based on swift, short passing. Unlike many traditional English sides, his team was built on a fundamental reliance on possession, mirroring the way in which other European sides had been playing for years. His teams could still mix it up, if necessary. Players like Tommy Smith, captain Emlyn Hughes, Ray Kennedy and Jimmy Case could all look after themselves if a scrappy game broke out.

That was Shankly's ethos; his successor, Paisley, was perhaps more tactically sophisticated. Certainly his core midfield of Case, McDermott, Callaghan and Kennedy was the perfect mix of talent, application and discipline. Like the great total football sides, there

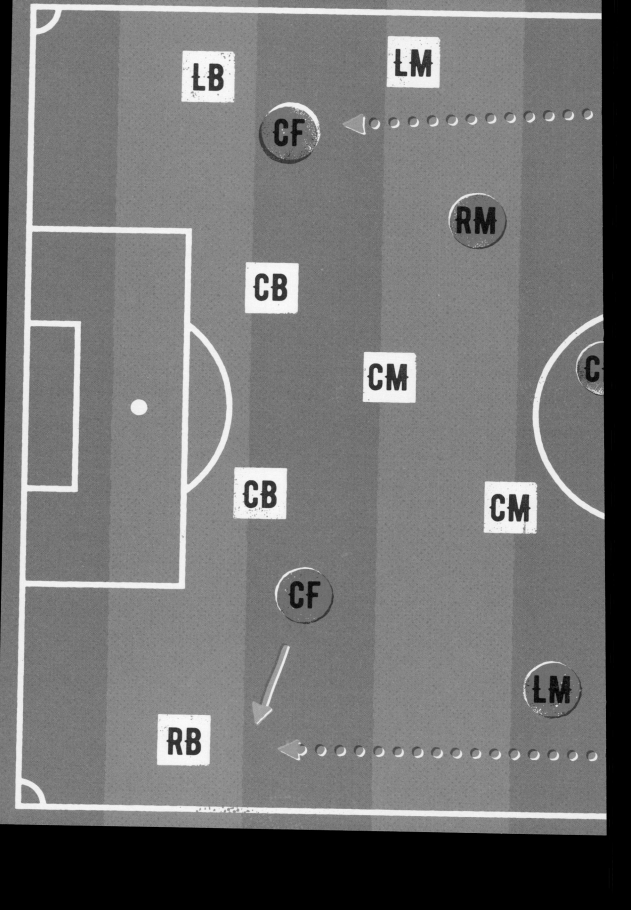

RB

FINDING SPACE

●	Liverpool
□	Borussia Mönchengladbach
→	Movement of player
•••▶	Passing moves

CB

CF

CM

CB

Typical Liverpool action involved playing the ball long down the wings and into a largely undefended midfield.

LB

Key Player

So much of what was great about this Liverpool side was typified by Kevin Keegan. The player, who stood under 178 cm, was surprisingly good in the air and used his combination of strength and speed to be a permanent nuisance to the German defence. With Keegan, Liverpool could encourage the team's midfielders to make runs into the opposition penalty area, confident in the knowledge that the striker had pulled opposition players out of position with his unselfish running.

was a trust that would allow someone like McDermott to break past the forward line to score that opening goal in Rome. All players ahead of the defenders shared the responsibility of scoring and contributing assists. And the fact that his forward players were so flexible with their movement, meant that the likes of Keegan (a future Ballon D'Or winner) and Heighway were creators as well as finishers.

Paisley's Liverpool were slightly more circumspect than Shankly's, and placed a premium on strong defence. In the 1978–79 season, the team conceded just four goals at home all season in the league – a forty-two-game campaign. Paisley also had the ability to spot the right player to replace one leaving the squad. His team of 1978 showed three key changes: Graeme Souness and Alan Hansen played key roles in future Red sides, as did Kenny Dalglish. Selected to replace Keegan, Dalglish ended up surpassing him.

Although we have chosen this first European Cup for analysis, it is instructive to look at Liverpool teams of the future, who continued to win league titles and European Cups with line-ups that seldom changed formation. At their core was hard work and application, pioneered by those three Scots. In future years, teams tried to replicate Liverpool's counter-pressing style, allied to their sharpness of attack and clinical finishing. That would be improved by the acquisition of

Liverpool's front six players worked in such a way that they could interchange positions, each equally capable of creating or scoring.

Ian Rush, a striker with predatory instincts, but who also offered the side its first line of defence with relentless harrying of the opposition. The sight of him running down defenders in possession of the ball was akin to watching Keegan plaguing Borussia's defence.

Perhaps the final assessment of the Liverpool team of this era is that it had borrowed parts of whatever made other sides great. The team utilised every one of its players to attack like the greats of Ajax and the Netherlands and defended stoutly like the Italians (the players' use of the back-pass rule could kill a game with plenty remaining). In their day, Liverpool could play with a flair rarely seen in the English league. Was it the system or was it the players? Or was it the management? It was a combination of the three, a fact that made this side the dominant English team of the late 1970s and 1980s.

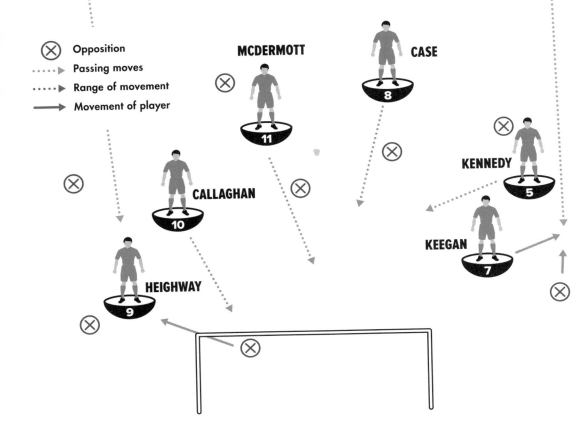

⊗ Opposition
····▷ Passing moves
····▷ Range of movement
──▶ Movement of player

MCDERMOTT CASE

KENNEDY

CALLAGHAN

KEEGAN

HEIGHWAY

THE ITALIAN JOB

6

HOW SACCHI AND CAPELLO CHANGED FOOTBALL FOREVER

THE MATCH

AC MILAN 4–0 BARCELONA

Champions League Final
18 May 1994
Olympiakó Stádio, Athens, Greece

THE ITALIAN JOB

6

HOW SACCHI AND CAPELLO CHANGED FOOTBALL FOREVER

The dominance of English clubs in Europe came to a halt when they were banned from European competitions after the Heysel Stadium disaster in 1985. The ban was not lifted for five years, with Liverpool serving an extra year, clearing the way for another team to take the lead. AC Milan, all-powerful in the 1960s, had since fallen on hard times and, by 1986, were barely mentioned when the conversation turned to top clubs on the Continent. That is, until club owner Silvio Berlusconi decided to appoint an unknown manager.

AC MILAN 4–0 BARCELONA

CHAMPIONS LEAGUE FINAL, 18 MAY 1994
OLYMPIAKÓ STÁDIO, ATHENS, ATTENDANCE 70,000

Arrigo Sacchi took the reins in 1987, having impressed in a two-year spell at Parma. In his first season, he helped Milan win the Serie A title, propelling the Rossoneri to back-to-back European Cup victories. Milan were blessed with great talent in the form of their Dutch trio: Ruud Gullit, Marco van Basten and Frank Rijkaard. In defence, they

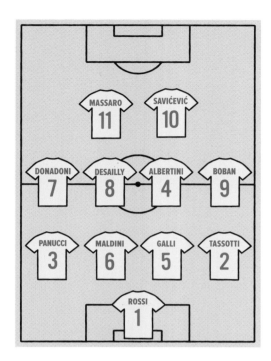

AC MILAN

GK	1	Sebastiano Rossi
RB	2	Mauro Tassotti (captain)
CB	5	Filippo Galli
CB	6	Paolo Maldini
LB	3	Christian Panucci
RW	9	Zvonimir Boban
CM	4	Demetrio Albertini
CM	8	Marcel Desailly
LM	7	Roberto Donadoni
CF	10	Dejan Savićević
CF	11	Daniele Massaro

Manager Fabio Capello

BARCELONA

GK	1	Andoni Zubizarreta
RB	2	Albert Ferrer
CB	4	Ronald Koeman
CB	5	Miguel Angel Nadal
LB	7	Sergi Barjuán
CM	3	Pep Guardiola
CM	9	Guillermo Amor
CM	6	José Mari Bakero (captain)
RW	8	Hristo Stoichkov
CF	10	Romário
LW	11	Txiki Begiristain

Manager Johan Cruyff

had wonderful balance with the likes of the experienced Franco Baresi and the youthful Paolo Maldini. Sacchi left the team in 1991, to be succeeded by another Italian, Fabio Capello. One of the most successful managers of all time, Capello brought four Serie A titles to the San Siro. He oversaw a change in personnel, sidelining the Dutch players previously favoured and introducing new talents Marcel Desailly and Zvonimir Boban. Capello's real skill was in maintaining a winning formula at a time when the Italian league was at its strongest. The nation had reached the World Cup Final in 1994 and, during this era, Juventus, Sampdoria and Parma all had strong teams.

In Barcelona, under the tutelage of Johan Cruyff, the Catalan giants had won four successive La Liga titles and their first European Cup. Known as the 'Dream Team', this side contained hall-of-famers that included Michael Laudrup, Romário, Hristo Stoichkov, Gheorghe Hagi and Ronald Koeman. In the league, they had scored ninety-one goals and were one of the most complete attacking outfits ever seen.

The only issue for both sides was the rule, implemented by UEFA in 1991, that teams could only field three foreign players in their starting line-ups. It meant that the Laudrup brothers (Michael and Brian) were left out of the Barcelona and Milan sides respectively.

The Match

In Athens, Milan began with their trademark 4–4–2 formation, honed under Sacchi, while Barcelona favoured a 4–3–3 with Pep Guardiola acting as a shield in front of the back four. Given the much-vaunted nature of Cruyff's attack, the front three created very little. Guillermo Amor came closest, with a shot that was thwarted by Filippo Galli. Shortly after, Milan took the lead through Daniele Massaro, who volleyed home a cross from Dejan Savićević.

Milan deserved their lead – they had been first to every ball during the opening quarter of the game, with Barcelona too casual in possession and appearing leaden footed. The goal had come from Bakero not paying enough attention to the strength and persistence of Savićević, who ran towards goal after Boban had dispossessed Sergi and fed him the ball.

It was noticeable that Milan's players were bigger than the Catalans, using their size to marginalise Barcelona's skillful but smaller forwards. The Milan team also varied its attacks. Sometimes players attacked centrally, at other times the threat came from wide areas. Barcelona started to threaten more in the closing stages of the first half and Romário took a shot that was deflected behind. However, deep into the first half's injury time, Milan doubled their lead. Roberto Donadoni dribbled past Albert Ferrer on the Milan left and raced for the byline. His accurate pull back was met by a ferocious shot that flew past Andoni Zubizarreta. Already, it seemed that coming back from this was beyond Barcelona. The whistle blew shortly after that goal and the stats show that Barcelona had more than 55 per cent possession, but had obviously failed to use it effectively.

Milan dominated the midfield, passing quickly and accurately for a more fluid advance.

Two minutes into the second half, Savićević put the game to bed. He had tormented Bakero all night and, after robbing him on the edge of the Barcelona penalty area, he produced the most audacious

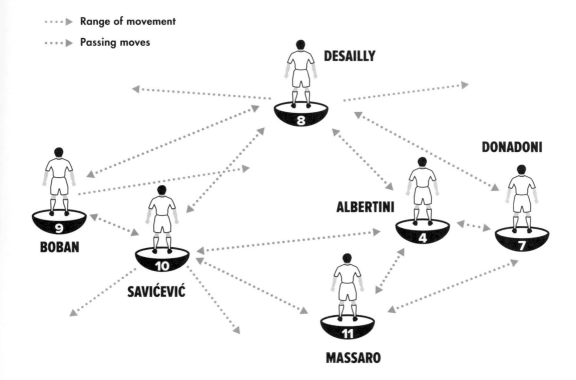

···▶ **Range of movement**

···▶ **Passing moves**

DESAILLY

8

DONADONI

ALBERTINI

BOBAN

9

4

7

SAVIĆEVIĆ

10

MASSARO

11

FORCEFUL ATTACK

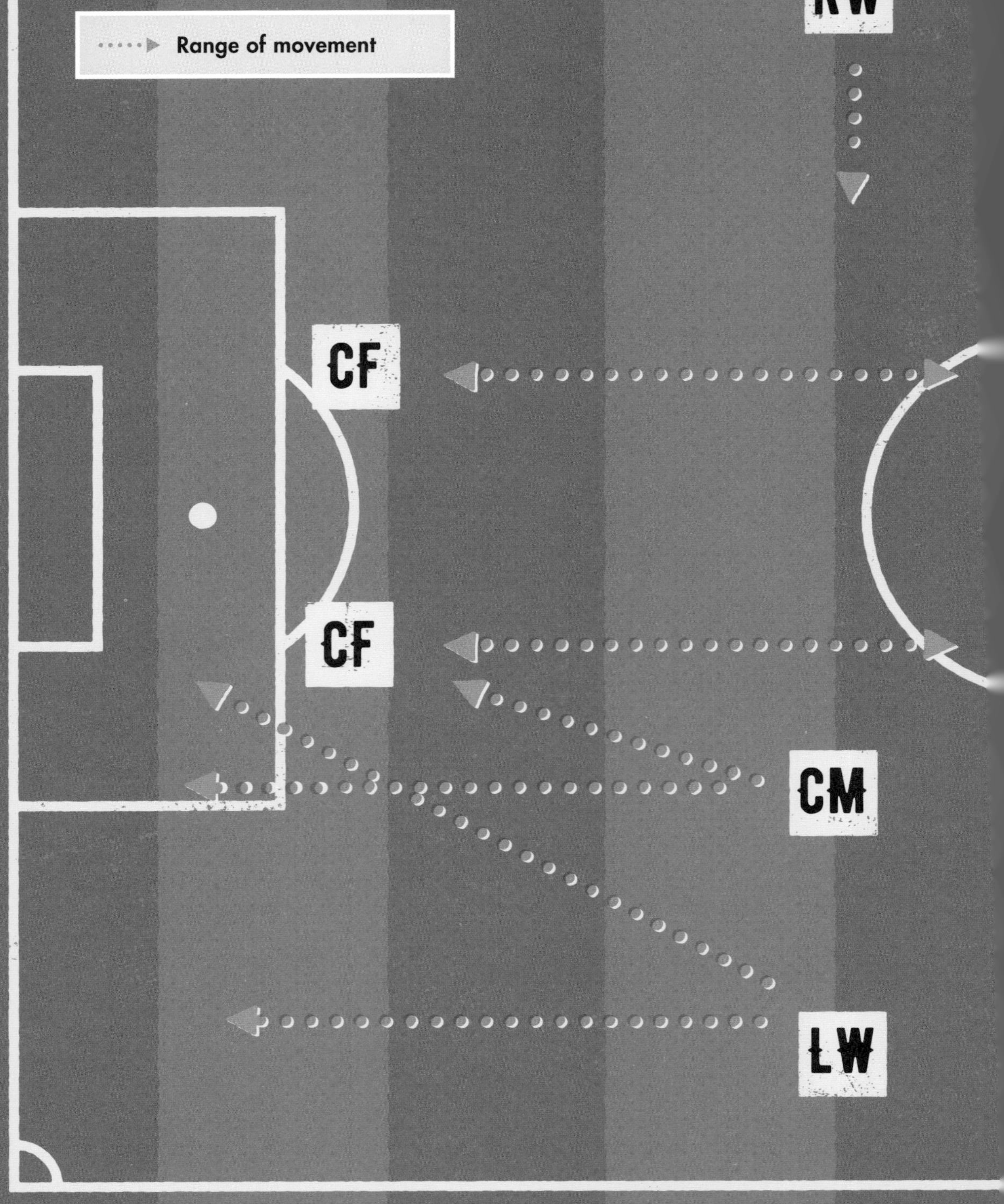

Range of movement

RW

CF

CF

CM

LW

On the attack, Capello's tactic relied on a holding midfielder – in Milan's case, Desailly – to feed the ball forward. Ahead of him, the forwards frequently interchanged positions.

M

lob to beat Zubizarreta. Yet the team's crowning glory was still to come. In the fifty-eighth minute, Desailly stormed through broken play forty yards from goal, took the neatest of short passes from Demetrio Albertini and slotted a right-footed shot of exquisite curl into the net. Capello, who had been restrained in his jubilation after each goal, allowed himself an embrace from his assistants.

For Barcelona, this was the end of an era. The team had to wait four years before another league title and twelve for its next European Cup Final. But for Milan, this was proof of the team's standing as the best in Europe. Three titles in the space of six years, under two different managers, and with a style of play that had not previously been associated with Italian football.

Desailly's goal showed how Milan made the most of their high-pressing tactics, with Albertini forcing Barcelona to bungle their defending.

The Philosophy

The change in the way Milan played football began under Arrigo Sacchi. It wasn't easy for him to convince all of his players to buy into what he was doing, least of all the three Dutchmen in his camp who, true to their football upbringing, had their own thoughts on how football should be played.

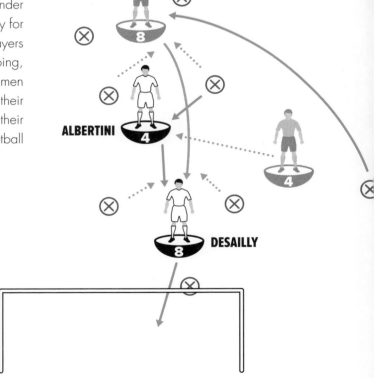

⊗   **Opposition**

····▶   **Range of movement**

⟶   **Movement of player**

⟶   **Pass**

What should have satisfied them was the knowledge that Sacchi's inspiration came from two sources, one of them being Dutch total football. The other was catenaccio, a method that had been successful for the great Inter Milan side during the 1960s. Sacchi wanted to marry these two polar opposites. To demonstrate this, he organised a defence-versus-attack training initiative in which five defensive players, including the goalkeeper, took on ten attackers. The objective was for the five to prevent the ten from scoring during a fifteen-minute period. They were always successful. Sacchi also staged games between two sets of players, but without a football, inviting them to take positions across the pitch when he told them where the ball might be. This Milan side defended zonally instead of following classic man-to-man marking. They also pressed high up the pitch, aggressively seeking to retrieve the ball.

'It was total football but it had balance. Italian identity means there will always be balance defensively. What he had were players who were very talented but also intelligent, who could take instructions. Everyone took part in the movement, whether it was going forward or backward. They had total intelligence. They knew how to adapt given the circumstances.' *Italian football journalist, Mina Rzouki*

Sacchi never wanted his defence and midfield to be more than twenty-five metres apart. It was the kind of football that drew compliments from the very best: 'He changed Italian football. He got rid of catenaccio by proposing a high-pressing game, with Maldini pushing forward on the flank. The Italian mentality was to attack with caution. Then all of a sudden there was no more catenaccio, but a four-man defence, with a side that attacked, rather than waited to counter-attack. It was a great change', said Sir Alex Ferguson.

Capello's Milan were similar in many ways, and he had an eye for a player. Desailly was a defender when he signed him, but was employed as a central, holding midfielder to great effect. During that convincing win over Barcelona, he was part of a midfield that pressed the life out of the opposition.

COMPACT DEFENCE

AC Milan
Barcelona

LB

RW

CB

CM

CF

CM

CM

GK

CB

LW

RB

In defence, Milan adopted a 4–1–4–1 formation –
a tactic that meant they conceded just two goals
in the eight games leading to this final.

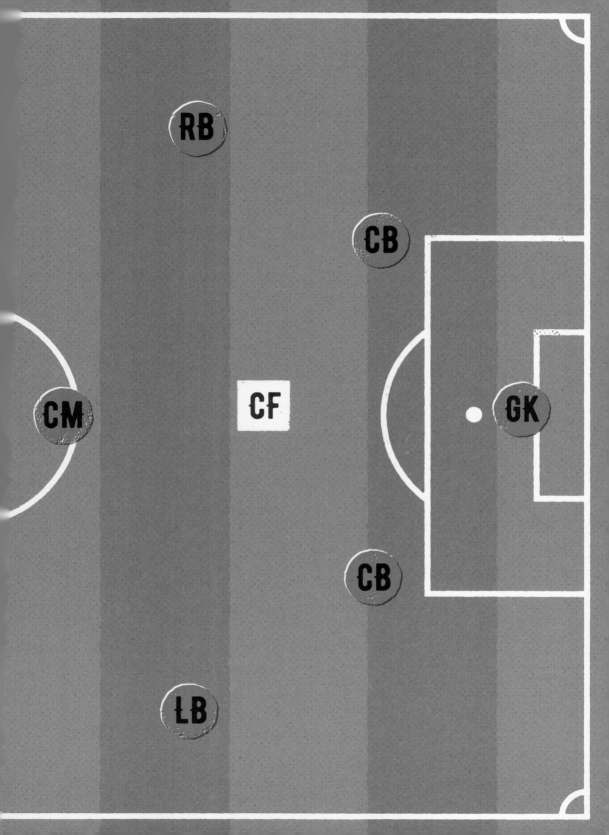

Key Player

Marcel Desailly's worth to this side was manifold. His ability to screen the defence and allow the formation of the whole team to move from a 4–4–2 to a 4–1–4–1 allowed the side great fluidity and flexibility and to surprise the opposition with changes in its patterns of play. And his fast, muscular presence helped to quell any potential uprising from a becalmed Barcelona.

In his autobiography, Barcelona coach Johan Cruyff hints at the fact that his side was still recovering from winning the La Liga title four days earlier, but any perceived tiredness was exaggerated by Milan's style. It can be found in all four of their goals. From the first, when Boban pressed Sergi into losing the ball and fed the high-energy Savićević, through to the fourth, where Albertini harried Barcelona in midfield and fed Desailly with a pass that allowed him to run through and finish the game. The collective intelligence was such that Albertini knew it was worth pressing high to force another mistake from Barcelona. It also relied upon Desailly forsaking his much deeper position to make the run.

Squeezing space on the pitch suffocated Barcelona's normally fluid passing and movement. Capello had identified that the team could only work so freely if its players were allowed the time and space to do so. The likes of Ronald Koeman and Pep Guardiola were forced into conceding possession or losing passes because of the strong pressing of the Milan forwards as well as the team's rigorous shape. The performance delivered so many of the things the coach demanded of his players, he was moved to say it was 'perfection'.

'Wherever you go, you have to be absolutely convinced about your vision of football. You have to look closely at the players you have, analyse them and know how to bring the very best out of every single one. How do you do that? By finding a playing style, a system, that allows the players to produce their best and by demanding that they make the greatest effort', said the Italian in later years.

Capello also identified that the pressing style he favoured, which had begun under Sacchi, required a fresh injection of personnel on a regular basis. At the end of every season, he would tweak his side based on using younger, fresher players in key positions. One such player was Desailly, for whom the formation could change. The shielding role in 4–4–2 could easily become 4–1–4–1, with the Frenchman sitting in front of the defence and one of the forwards withdrawing into a deeper number 10 role.

Bear in mind one final thing – this system, combining Sacchi's high-tempo pressing and Capello's tactical tweaks – survived the absence of two pivotal defensive figures in the 1994 final: Franco Baresi and Alessandro Costacurta, the regular central defenders, were suspended. An incredibly high level of collective intelligence and trust coursed through the veins of every Milan player for this short period of time.

Milan starved Barcelona's strikers of the ball, blocking passing lanes with two banks of four players.

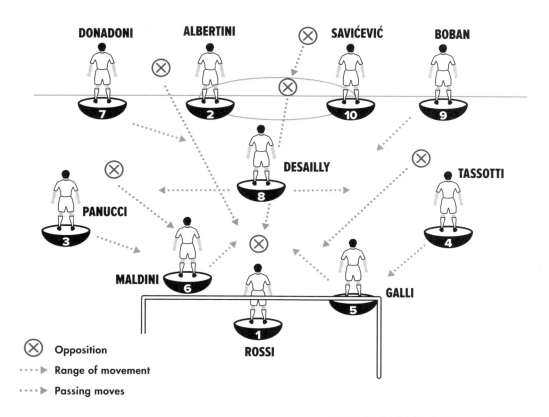

DONADONI   ALBERTINI   SAVIĆEVIĆ   BOBAN

7   2   10   9

DESAILLY

8

PANUCCI   TASSOTTI

3   4

MALDINI   GALLI

6   5

ROSSI   1

⊗ Opposition
····▶ Range of movement
····▶ Passing moves

7

THE FRENCH REVOLUTION

THE MATCH

FRANCE 3–0 BRAZIL

World Cup Final
12 July 1998
Stade de France, Paris, France

THE FRENCH REVOLUTION

Having failed to qualify for the World Cup in 1990 and 1994, France gained an automatic qualification in the 1998 tournament, as they were hosts. The generations of players who had failed to get their hands on the trophy included Michel Platini, Éric Cantona and Just Fontaine – one of the tournament's all-time top scorers.

FRANCE 3-0 BRAZIL

WORLD CUP FINAL, 12 JULY 1998
STADE DE FRANCE, PARIS, ATTENDANCE 80,000

Aside from a strong Marseille side in the early 1990s – winners of France's only Champions League victory – the country was better known for players who plied their trade around the world. Of the starting eleven for this World Cup Final, only two players were based in France. The other nine played for such clubs as Real Madrid, Juventus and Inter Milan. Crucially, one of those players was Zinedine Zidane, whose impressive performances for a resurgent Juventus had not gone unnoticed.

Having conceded just two goals on its way to the final, the French team was considered defensively sound. The Brazilians, meanwhile, were once again drawing plaudits for their cavalier nature. They

FRANCE

GK	16	Fabien Barthez
RB	15	Lilian Thuram
CB	18	Frank Leboeuf
CB	8	Marcel Desailly
LB	3	Bixente Lizarazu
CM	19	Christian Karembeu
DM	7	Didier Deschamps (captain)
CM	17	Emmanuel Petit
AM	6	Youri Djorkaeff
AM	10	Zinedine Zidane
CF	9	Stéphane Guivarc'h

Manager Aimé Jacquet

BRAZIL

GK	1	Claudio Taffarel
RB	2	Cafu
CB	3	Aldair
CB	4	Júnior Baiano
LB	6	Roberto Carlos
CM	5	César Sampaio
CM	8	Dunga (captain)
AM	10	Rivaldo
AM	18	Leonardo
CF	20	Bebeto
CF	9	Ronaldo

Manager Mário Zagallo

had scored thirteen goals en route to Paris and, with the talents of Ronaldo, Rivaldo, Bebeto and Roberto Carlos, it was widely believed they would be too strong for France. An obvious chink in the team's armour was its defence – Brazil had let in six goals on their way to the final and had needed extra time and penalties to see off the Netherlands in a gruelling semi-final.

On the day of the match, there emerged speculation that Ronaldo might not be able to play for Brazil, having suffered convulsions in his hotel room. He had scored four goals and created three on his way to the final, but such was the worry over his state of health that evening, that he was removed from the team line-up and reinstated just before kickoff. At his best, the striker was unrivalled, a blend of pace, power and skill that may never be matched again. Brazil were considered favourites as four-time winners of the trophy and the reigning champions. Virtually all of the players played in Europe, so conditions were not unfamiliar to them. Several had been part of the side that had won the cup in the United States four years earlier. In charge of them was legendary coach Mário Zagallo, while France had the relatively unknown Aimé Jacquet.

The Match

France dominated the early stages of the game. They seemed able to turn the Brazil defence around by mixing up the way they played, either by hitting long vertical passes for Stéphane Guivarc'h or concentrating on set pieces, where they could unpick the opposition's back four. Through luck and bad finishing, the scores were level when Brazil threatened briefly through a shot/cross from Roberto Carlos that forced Fabien Barthez to make a save. Shortly after, Barthez had to hold on when Brazil took a free header from a corner.

It was from a disputed corner of their own that France took the lead in the twenty-seventh minute. Emmanuel Petit swung the ball in to Zidane, who sent a header down past Claudio Taffarel. There was relief all around the Stade de France – Zidane's goal was courtesy of a good delivery from Petit and his own ability to rise higher than the Brazilian defence.

Petit almost added a second in the fortieth minute. A rebound fell to him, but on his weaker right foot, and he pushed a looping shot just wide of the post. But a second goal was not far off. Guivarc'h had a shot brilliantly saved by Taffarel, from a corner, in first-half injury time; from the other side of the pitch, Zidane withdrew from the goal line and was completely unmarked when he headed in the second goal.

Predictably, the second half began with Brazil having plenty of the ball. But there was some scrappy play, often involving Desailly, who picked up a contentious yellow card three minutes into the half, and a second when he charged up the pitch on a counter-attack that seemed destined to fail and scythed down Cafu. France, already

Typical attacking strategy was to keep the ball central, while the full backs made great runs up and down the wings.

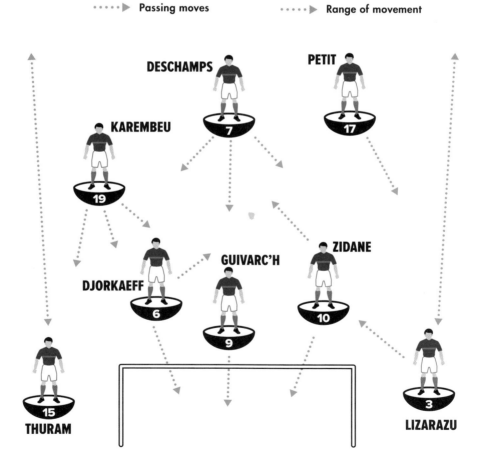

······▷ **Passing moves**   ······▷ **Range of movement**

THE CHRISTMAS TREE

LB

CM

CB

GK

DM

CB

CM

RB

France's formation — sometimes called the Christmas tree — hinged on the three central players directing play, and moving the ball forward centrally, rather than down the wings.

AM

AM

CF

sitting deep and defending resolutely, dropped a few yards deeper. To compensate for the loss of Desailly, Lilian Thuram moved from right back to the centre before Petit moved into the vacated position.

Brazil committed to attack as well, with Denílson and Edmundo on to replace two midfielders. But the pattern of play remained the same: Brazil had a lot of the ball and France broke up attacks thirty yards from goal. There was still time for the crowning glory – Brazil took a corner and committed every man forward, but France broke away quickly. Leading the attack, Christophe Dugarry passed to another substitute, Patrick Vieira, who immediately rolled the ball into the path of Petit who made it 3–0 in the final minute of injury time. France were World Champions for the first time ever. They won the European Cup two years later, with a golden-goal victory over Italy in the final.

The Philosophy

Such was the fluidity of the French team during the final that its formation changed frequently. What was amazing was that, in the form of Zidane and Youri Djorkaeff, the French coach Aimé Jacquet

In defence, France's three forwards were responsible for preventing Dunga passing through the centre.

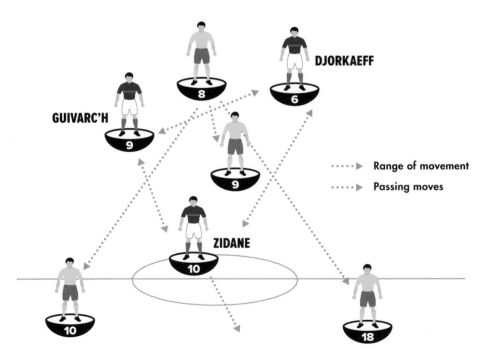

GUIVARC'H 9

DJORKAEFF 6

8

9

ZIDANE 10

10

18

⋯⋯▶ **Range of movement**
⋯⋯▶ **Passing moves**

chose to use those two players as artisans as much as artists. Zidane played as a marauding attacker, working between midfield and the two players ahead of him. This kept pressure on Brazil's Dunga, who liked to take the ball from his defence and feed players ahead of him, who were more capable. If the ball was in French possession, Zidane could supplement his side's attack but as soon as the ball was lost, his job was to block Dunga's view when surveying his options.

Djorkaeff helped in this respect, and was also not averse to taking the ball out of the congested centre and dribbling into areas where he could not harm, but simply make sure that Brazil did not have the ball. This meant that France's obvious outlet was through the middle and it was staggering to see how often the players were able to find Guivarc'h with hopeful passes. While the team started in a 4–3–2–1 formation, it easily became 4–4–2 or 4–3–3 depending on what suited at the time.

'It was more of a group team than putting an emphasis on individual players. Jacquet always put defence ahead of attack. And after the World Cup, the domestic teams progressed with that formula. Having said that, his training sessions were more about mentality than tactics, so they could excute what he wanted on the pitch. I'd say his brand of football was a combination of English mentality and Italian steel.' *French football journalist, Loïc Tanzi*

Jacquet's tactics worked because Brazil adhered to a much narrower style. They lined up in a 4–2–2–2 formation, with a great distance between the midfield pair of Dunga and César Sampaio and the wingers, Leonardo and Rivaldo. This allowed Zidane and Djorkaeff to press the space more effectively. The out ball that France used was less effective with the slight Bebeto up front and a diffident Ronaldo who was clearly not the player of the early rounds.

But pressing wasn't the only aspect of the game in which France were superior. The reason they were able to play the out ball to Guivarc'h was the distance between Brazil's goalkeeper and the backline. The unit was not as compact as France's, where Barthez,

IMPENETRABLE DEFENCE

ŁB

AM

CF

CB

DM

CB

CF

AM

RB

When defending, France adopted a 4–3–3 formation, with the three midfielders helping to create two impenetrable lines.

RB

M

AM

CB

CF

CM

AM

CB

LB

Key Player

It is impossible to overstate the importance of Zinedine Zidane. As the one Frenchman who could match skills and flair with the best of the Brazilians, his ability to deliver a performance of style and grace was paramount. Aside from his goals, he played a key role in making sure that Brazil were unable to control the tempo of the game. Emmanuel Petit and Lilian Thuram also deserve credit. The former held his shape in defence and attacked to great effect, with an assist and a goal, while the latter patrolled his side's right flank in tandem with Christian Karembeu and provided a useful outlet with his strong running.

who could also function as a sweeper-keeper, helped to squeeze more available space out of the reach of Brazil – the slightest room between the defensive line and the keeper would have been exploited by Ronaldo's blistering pace.

Brazil tried to change the rhythm of the game by switching to a 3–3–4 formation, with Dunga almost playing as a sweeper in a back three and the full backs absorbed into midfield. But France merely changed shape to become more compact, with the midfield and attack becoming two banks of three. That change required Brazil's second central midfielder, César Sampaio, to play a more expansive game – something he could not get to grips with.

Of course, France were tested during the final quarter of the game, once Desailly had been sent off. But Brazil's play was becoming increasingly desperate, their passing too direct as space between the full backs and the central defenders was difficult to find. Even the introduction of Denílson, a genuine winger with pace, did not help them become more progressive. For the whole game, Brazil had failed to find penetration down the flanks, despite having the likes of Roberto Carlos and soon-to-be Player of the Year, Rivaldo. They were thwarted by the organisation of France, who on the right flank, with Karembeu and Thuram, were surprisingly untroubled.

When adopting a defensive formation, one of the two central midfielders would hold the centre line with Deschamps, while the other advanced to be ready for a counter-attack.

What Jacquet and other coaches of his ilk did was to encourage other teams during the following years to believe that organisation, good defence and hard work were enough to be competitive. A score of 3–0 might have indicated total dominance, yet that was not exactly the case. But France were the better side in both attack and defence. Although the team was packed with players who went on to become legends of the game, notably Zidane, in 1998 it was considered just 'very good'. However, their collective approach made Jacquet's gameplan of maintaining defensive solidity and taking advantage of Brazil's shortcomings work most effectively.

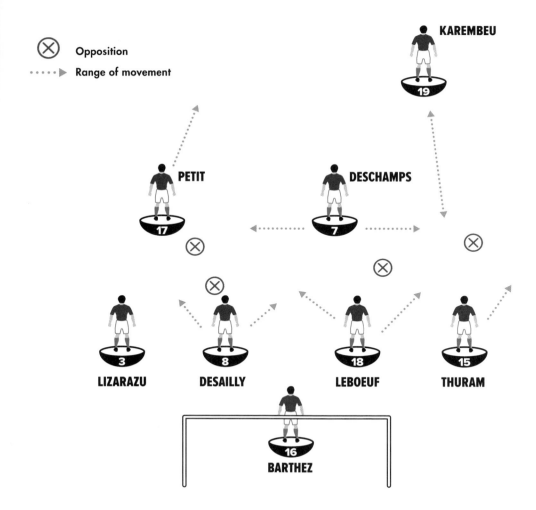

A MAN FROM GOVAN

8

THE MATCH

MANCHESTER UNITED 1–1 CHELSEA
(6–5 on penalties)

Champions League Final
21 May 2008
Luzhniki, Moscow, Russia

A MAN FROM GOVAN

Rating Manchester United in terms of just one game between 1986 and 2013 is impossible. Those twenty-seven years under Sir Alex Ferguson saw the team go from perennial underachievers to the dominant side in England. During that time, the man from the Govan district of Glasgow, Scotland, oversaw one thousand games and masterminded thirteen Premier League title-winning campaigns, two Champions Leagues and nine domestic cups.

What set Ferguson apart was a commitment to exciting and penetrative football from his midfield. His first Premier League title-winning side saw a midfield of Andrei Kanchelskis, Paul Ince, Bryan Robson and a teenage Ryan Giggs tear the opposition apart within minutes. Ahead of that quartet played Mark Hughes, Brian McClair and the great Éric Cantona. With goals flowing from all angles, thirty-five came from attack and twenty from midfield.

It is often thought that Ferguson's early sides adopted a conventional 4–4–2 formation, but there was greater sophistication than that. The front pair occupied two very different positions in a 4–4–1–1, with Hughes as the spearhead of the attack and either Cantona or McClair in a slightly withdrawn role. A withdrawing striker allowed others to advance from midfield.

Ferguson's all-conquering side won league titles in 1993, 1994, 1996 and 1997, but continually came up short in European competition. To some extent English teams were still playing catch-up with their European counterparts, having been exiled from European football for five years following the 1985 Heysel Stadium disaster. During that time, the game had become more focused on possession and the world's best players were in Spain and Italy. A dynamic counter-pressing side, such as United, was less effective when starved of possession for extended periods. But, by 1999, Ferguson had built a squad that could act outside the fast counter-pressing style that was so effective in England, with centre backs more suited to mainland European football and an array of midfield options – from the explosive (Ryan Giggs) to the subtle and silky (David Beckham) – who were able to go blow for blow with some of Europe's big hitters. United drew twice with a very strong Barcelona in the group stage of that year's Champions League and beat Inter Milan and Juventus to get to the final. There, they came from behind to beat Bayern Munich 2–1, scoring both goals in injury time.

League titles accumulated over the next four years, but Ferguson was forced to break up the side that had brought him so much success, and between 1999 and 2008, only a handful of players (Gary Neville, Paul Scholes, Wes Brown and Ryan Giggs) remained. Nevertheless, Ferguson's squad was the envy of many sides across Europe, particularly in the forward areas. A front two of Carlos Tevez and Wayne Rooney was complemented by a blossoming Cristiano Ronaldo, signed by Ferguson at the age of 18 in a deal that, at the time, made him the most expensive teenager in English football. At first glimpse, he appeared to be all tricks, but that soon changed as he added muscle to his frame and goals to his repertoire.

MANCHESTER UNITED

GK	1	Edwin van der Sar
RB	6	Wes Brown
CB	5	Rio Ferdinand (captain)
CB	15	Nemanja Vidić
LB	3	Patrice Evra
CM	18	Paul Scholes
CM	16	Michael Carrick
RM	4	Owen Hargreaves
LM	7	Cristiano Ronaldo
CF	10	Wayne Rooney
CF	32	Carlos Tevez

Manager Sir Alex Ferguson

CHELSEA

GK	1	Petr Cech
RB	5	Michael Essien
CB	6	Ricardo Carvalho
CB	26	John Terry (captain)
LB	3	Ashley Cole
DM	4	Claude Makélélé
CM	13	Michael Ballack
CM	8	Frank Lampard
RW	10	Joe Cole
CF	11	Didier Drogba
LW	15	Florent Malouda

Manager Avram Grant

MANCHESTER UNITED 1–1 CHELSEA

6–5 ON PENALTIES, CHAMPIONS LEAGUE FINAL, 21 MAY 2008
LUZHNIKI, MOSCOW, ATTENDANCE 67,310

Once again, United had faced Barcelona in their campaign to get to a Champions League final, gaining a 1–0 aggregate win over them in the penultimate stage. Chelsea's 4–3, two-leg victory over a resurgent Liverpool, meant the cup-winning side would be an English one. Chelsea were fearsome, built with investment from Roman Abramovich and the talent of José Mourinho, although the latter had left the club at the start of the campaign – in mutual agreement with Abramovich, their relationship having deteriorated. Chelsea were now coached by Avram Grant, who had helped the team push United all the way in the Premier League that season. They had some special players – keeper Petr Cech, defender John Terry, Claude Makélélé, Michael Ballack, Frank Lampard and Didier Drogba. Abramovich craved a side that could succeed with flair as well as the obvious power they possessed. A victory in the Champions League would be unique, especially since it was to take place in the owner's homeland.

United had faced various challenges under Ferguson: Blackburn Rovers, backed by owner-investor Jack Walker and skilfully managed by Kenny Dalglish; Arsène Wenger's dynamic Arsenal; and now Chelsea, financially sound, with a slew of top managers. Ferguson's response was always to rebuild and produce another side capable of glory. Was his current team the most complete?

The Match

Relentless rain was one of the abiding memories of this match. The day started with drizzle and ended with the kind of downpour that might have forced a cancellation but, with new stadiums better able to dry their turf after incessant rainfall, the game went ahead.

A DEFENSIVE MIDFIELD

● ● ● ► Range of movement

LB ● ● ● ● ● ● ● ● ● ● ● ● ● ● ●

CB

◄ ● ● ● ● ● ● ● ● ● ● **CM** ● ● ● ●

CB

◄ ● ● ● ● ● ● ● ● ● ● **CM** ● ● ● ●

RB ● ● ● ● ● ● ● ● ● ►

Manchester United played a 4–4–2 formation in which the two central midfielders, Scholes and Carrick could easily drop back to defend, while the wings held their width.

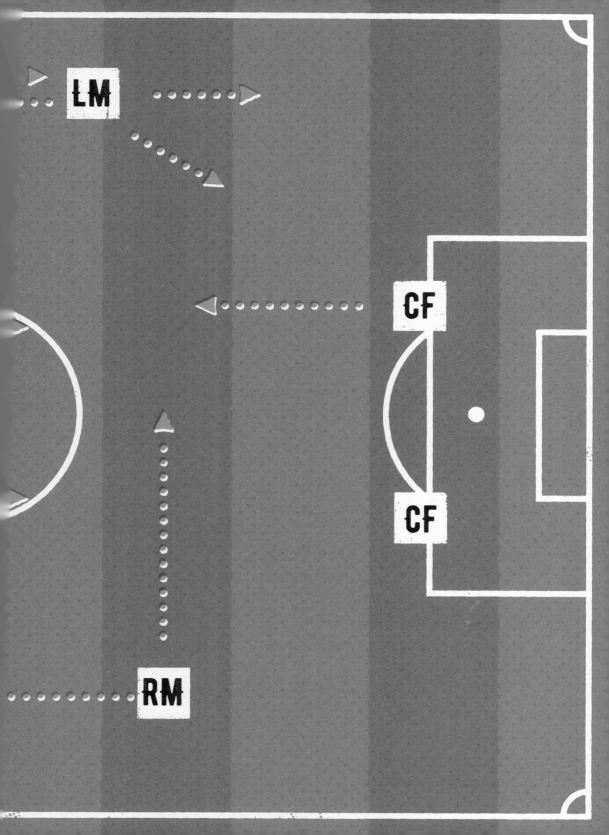

The first twenty minutes of this match were noteworthy only for a robust challenge from Paul Scholes on Claude Makélélé. The United midfielder may have been the most technically gifted player on the pitch, but tackling of any form was not his strength. In the twenty-sixth minute, United's Wes Brown, a player more comfortable as a centre back but playing as a right back, cut in from the wing and drifted a cross that found Cristiano Ronaldo on the edge of the six-yard box. The Portuguese player soared above Michael Essien (placed in a defensive position) to head past Petr Cech for the opening goal.

Apart from this event, no side had an obvious edge. The game was played in the middle of the pitch, with defenders holding their positions and putting in very comfortable blocks. But in the thirty-third minute, a long diagonal ball from Frank Lampard found Drogba pulling off from his markers to head back into the six-yard box. Michael Ballack, marked by Rio Ferdinand, was forced to head against his own crossbar.

Briefly, the game broke into an end-to-end contest, with Rooney dispossessing Ricardo Carvalho and spreading the play to Ronaldo on the left wing. A Rooney cross from the byline found a diving Carlos Tevez, whose header was brilliantly saved by Cech. The Chelsea goalkeeper then saved again, this time from Michael Carrick, who pounced on the ball. Once more, in the forty-second minute, Rooney drifted to the right wing, drilled a right-footed shot into the area, and the ball was just missed by a sliding Tevez.

The conditions deteriorated by the minute, and a pitch that had looked soft at the start was now very slippery and greasy – a fact that played a part in the equaliser, when a shot from Essien was deflected into the path of Lampard, who gently chipped the ball over Edwin van der Sar. The pitch had also made tackling difficult, as four yellow cards demonstrated.

The second half of the match was one in which defences held sway. Extra time seemed inevitable and Ferguson made his first change, replacing veteran Scholes with another man from the class of 1992, Ryan Giggs. United had to make the change, since Chelsea were looking stronger, especially on the wings. Both Florent Malouda and Joe Cole had produced crosses for Drogba – a threat that had only just been snuffed out by United's immaculate central defenders.

The extra period began with both sides looking tired and ready for more changes. Chelsea brought on Salomon Kalou and Nicolas Anelka for Malouda and Cole, while United replaced Rooney with another Portuguese winger, Nani. In the ninety-fourth minute, Lampard hit the underside of the crossbar with a left-footed shot. Giggs then had a point-blank shot headed over the bar by John Terry. With four minutes of the game remaining, Drogba was sent off for slapping Nemanja Vidić. Although the incident had no effect on the action, it changed the dynamic of the penalty shoot-out.

During the shoot-out, Chelsea had the chance to win the cup, but captain Terry slipped at the crucial moment and hit the post and Anelka had his effort saved by Van der Sar, so United won their third European Cup and their second under Sir Alex Ferguson.

Rooney's crosses proved dangerous on several occasions, with Tevez taking the right goalpost and Ronaldo the left.

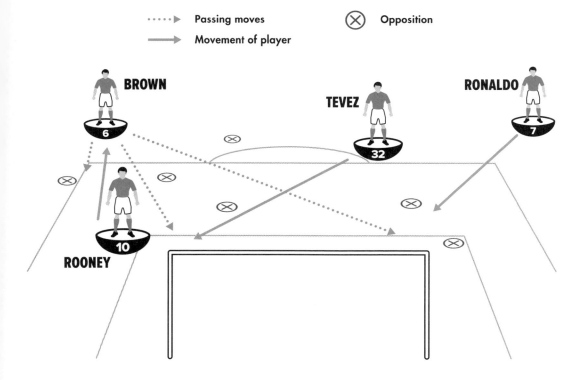

........▶ **Passing moves**   ⊗ **Opposition**

───────▶ **Movement of player**

BROWN

TEVEZ

RONALDO

ROONEY

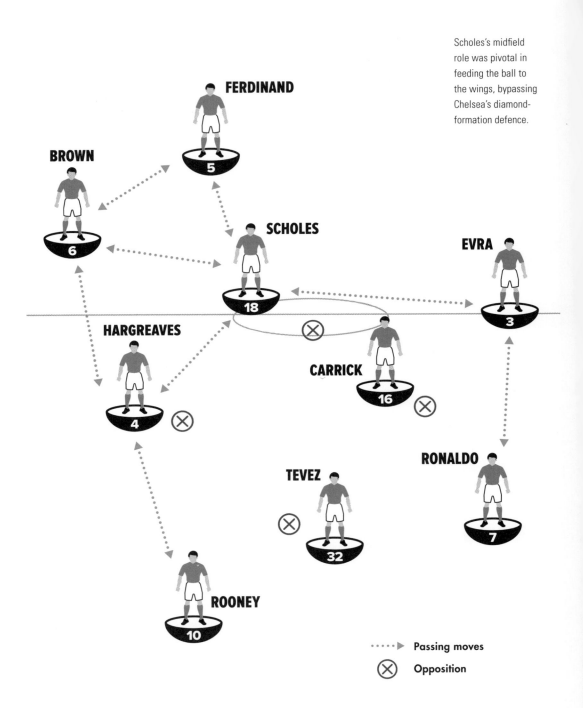

FERDINAND
5

BROWN
6

SCHOLES
18

EVRA
3

HARGREAVES
4

CARRICK
16

RONALDO
7

TEVEZ
32

ROONEY
10

Scholes's midfield role was pivotal in feeding the ball to the wings, bypassing Chelsea's diamond-formation defence.

· · · · ·▶ Passing moves

⊗ Opposition

The Philosophy

For the Moscow game, Sir Alex Ferguson reverted to a very conventional 4–4–2 formation, with Ronaldo and the versatile Owen Hargreaves as wingers. Up front were Rooney and Tevez, whose movement was almost impossible to anticipate, but the pair were more used to playing as a three, with Ronaldo as the third man. Ferguson's centre-back pairing of Rio Ferdinand and Nemanja Vidić offered a blend of elegance, power and pace that made for a frightening proposition for opposing managers. Since his early days at West Ham, Ferdinand had been praised for his elegance on the ball – a rare quality for an English defender. And alongside Vidić, he was playing with someone who always had his back.

'Defensively, they were exceptional,' says journalist Steven Wyeth, who covered United for five years. 'It was when Vidić and Ferdinand's partnership was in its absolute pomp. Van der Sar was one of the top three keepers in the world. Patrice Evra at left back was fantastic and at right back, he had the choice of either Wes Brown or John O'Shea. They knew each other's games and were just so well organised.'

The hallmark of Ferguson's great teams was a strong defensive unit. His first great side of the early 1990s had Peter Schmeichel in goal and a centre-back pairing of the combative Steve Bruce and elegant Gary Pallister. The treble-winning side of 1999 retained the goalkeeper and now had a maturing right back in Gary Neville, as well as the imposing Jakob 'Jaap' Stam. 'Along with the ideology to play bold and attacking football, there was always that solid platform', adds Wyeth. 'The best attacking players didn't necessarily win you the big prizes – you had to have defensive solidity.'

In this final, Ferguson opted for a midfield of intelligent screening in Michael Carrick – one of the most underrated players in British football, says Wyeth – and Scholes's elegant prompting. Some have opined that Ferguson got it wrong by playing Hargreaves as a right winger, but his prescence nullified the threat of Malouda for the first forty-five minutes. It was a tactical shift that allowed Rooney to drift into the right side of the pitch where he was comfortable. Although Ronaldo could be devastating through the middle or from either

WORKING THE LEFT FLANK

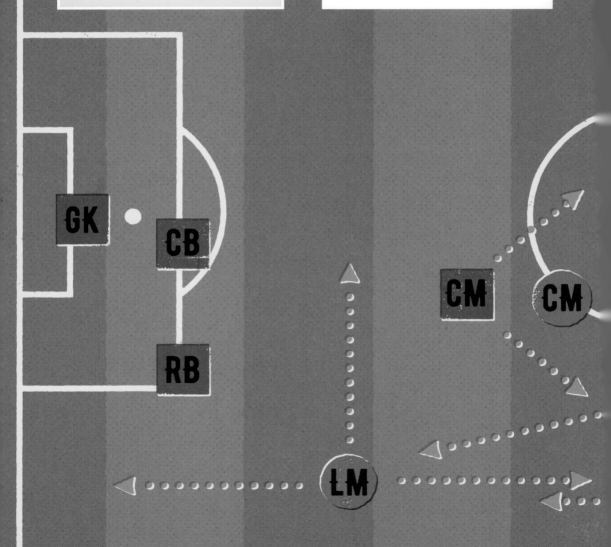

 Manchester United

 Chelsea

 Range of movement

With Evra and Ronaldo over- and underlapping one another, Manchester United frequently overloaded the left flank to stifle Chelsea's forward momentum, while creating chances of their own.

Key Player

Much of the team's tactical success came down to its defence. So tight were Rio Ferdinand and Nemanja Vidić at the back, that they helped Manchester United to win five league titles in just seven years. Of course, the team also benefitted from the explosive brilliance of Cristiano Ronaldo (Real Madrid paid a world-record fee for his services in 2009), while Edwin Van der Sar made the crucial save in the penalty shoot-out that won them the trophy.

flank, his starting position on the left exposed Chelsea's one genuine weakness at the right back. Michael Essien was a fearsome sight with pace and power to burn, but he was a midfielder converted to do a job for his team and his inexperience was obvious when he failed to challenge the Portuguese player for the opening goal. The plan had been to exploit this weakness, and although Chelsea would equalise and have chances thereafter, the team was never able to cut United open, even as tired limbs and muscles became an increasing factor during extra time.

United had suffered several defeats in European campaigns, knowing that they had gone out to teams that were not necessarily stronger, but were more adept at winning big games:

'Ferguson became aware that what was good enough to win the Premier League wasn't good enough in Europe . . . it was with assistant coach Carlos Queiroz that United started trying to experiment with things like three at the back or playing 4–1–3–2, using a midfield shield in front of the defence. They had to adapt if they were going to turn domestic success into European success.'
Steven Wyeth.

It might well have translated into even greater domination if United's rise in stature in the Champions League wasn't met by Barcelona's prominence. The sides met in two finals over the following three years and Pep Guardiola's side triumphed on both occasions.

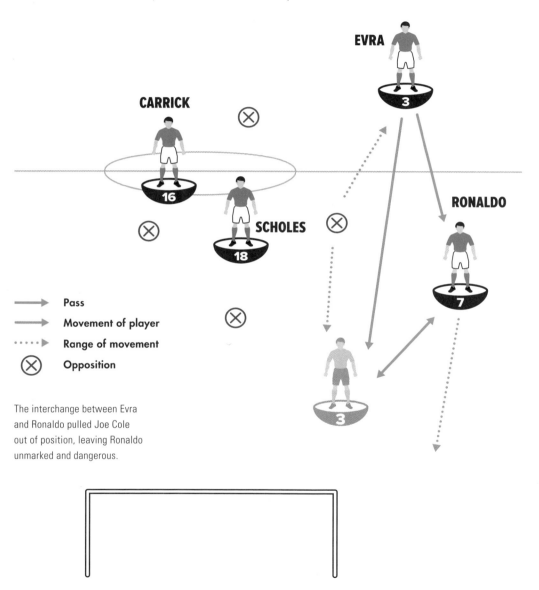

Pass

Movement of player

Range of movement

Opposition

The interchange between Evra and Ronaldo pulled Joe Cole out of position, leaving Ronaldo unmarked and dangerous.

TIKI TAKA: DEATH BY FOOTBALL

9

THE MATCH

SPAIN 1–0 NETHERLANDS

World Cup Final
11 July 2010
Soccer City Stadium,
Johannesburg, South Africa

BARCELONA 5–0 REAL MADRID

La Liga
29th November 2010
Camp Nou, Barcelona, Spain

TIKI TAKA: DEATH BY FOOTBALL

9

For a country that had given so much to football, it was amazing to think that, at the start of 2010, Spain had still not won a World Cup. Yet there was a feeling that this situation was about to change. The national side had been crowned European champions in 2008, after bamboozling nearly all other sides with a style that relied heavily on possession, but also featured the pure striking talents of David Silva and Fernando Torres. And the players had proved no less impressive since that tournament.

SPAIN 1-0 THE NETHERLANDS

WORLD CUP FINAL, 11 JULY 2010
SOCCER CITY STADIUM, JOHANNESBURG, ATTENDANCE 84,490

In all, Spain arrived at the 2010 World Cup having won forty-five of their previous forty-eight games, and having been victorious in all ten of their World Cup qualifying matches. A golden generation of players had emerged following a decade-long commitment to making sure that all Spanish players adhered to a style that was heavy on possession. Before now, a string of Spanish sides had reached big tournaments but had underachieved because the players struggled during difficult game situations.

SPAIN

GK	1	Iker Casillas (captain)
RB	15	Sergio Ramos
CB	3	Gerard Piqué
CB	5	Carles Puyol
LB	11	Joan Capdevila
DM	16	Sergio Busquets
DM	14	Xabi Alonso
CM	8	Xavi
RW	6	Andrés Iniesta
CF	7	David Villa
LW	18	Pedro

Manager Vicente del Bosque

THE NETHERLANDS

GK	1	Maarten Stekelenburg
RB	2	Gregory van der Wiel
CB	3	John Heitinga
CB	4	Joris Mathijsen
LB	5	Giovanni van Bronckhorst (captain)
DM	6	Mark van Bommel
DM	8	Nigel de Jong
RW	11	Arjen Robben
AM	10	Wesley Sneijder
LW	7	Dirk Kuyt
CF	9	Robin van Persie

Manager Bert van Marwijk

But this Spanish side was different. Not only did it contain several stars that had found success in European club competitions, it had also exported some of its best players to the more physically demanding English league. The team's coach, Vicente del Bosque, knew about pressure and the demands of a baying public, having spent four years at Real Madrid. So great are expectations at Santiago Bernabéu, that his manager's contract was not renewed, even after he had helped the side win another La Liga title in 2003. In 2008, he succeeded Luis Aragonés as Spain's head coach and brought an incredible amount of experience in dealing with a pressured environment, having managed the likes of Zidane, Figo and Ronaldo.

The fact that del Bosque hardly ever said anything – negative or positive – about his team or the opposition lent a certain mystique to his side. Was he quiet because he had so much faith in his side or was he quiet because that was his nature? The Spanish team lost its first game of the World Cup, a stunning 1–0 defeat by Switzerland. But it won the next two group games and got to the final having kept three clean sheets in the knockout stages, including a 1–0 victory over Germany in the semi-finals. It was felt that, if their defence could remain as miserly in the final against the Netherlands, then a first World Cup win would surely be theirs. Against the odds, the Dutch side had managed to reach its third final with stunning victories over Brazil and Uruguay. In Wesley Sneijder, the team had arguably the player of the tournament, and in Arjen Robben, they had the one player with genuine pace who could hurt Spain.

The Match

Cagey and aggressive is one way to describe this game, with most of the X-rated material coming from the Dutch, who were clearly keen to intimidate the Spanish physically during the early stages. In all, the Dutch committed twenty-eight fouls during play, many of them in the first half. Three players, Mark van Bommel, Nigel de Jong and Wesley Sneijder committed fouls of considerable brutality and were exceptionally fortunate not to have been sent off in the first half. The Dutch tactic of pressing the opposition high up the pitch was working after a strong start to the game from the Spanish. Spain had yet to unpick the Dutch defence, their best chances coming from set pieces.

Towards the end of the half, the Dutch started to sense that their tactics were having some success and Robben drew a save from Iker Casillas, but Spain were starting to have much more possession and the Dutch began to tire as the game progressed.

Both teams threatened from set pieces at the start of the second half but the real chance of the game came in the sixty-second minute, when a pass from Sneijder found an unmarked Robben sprinting

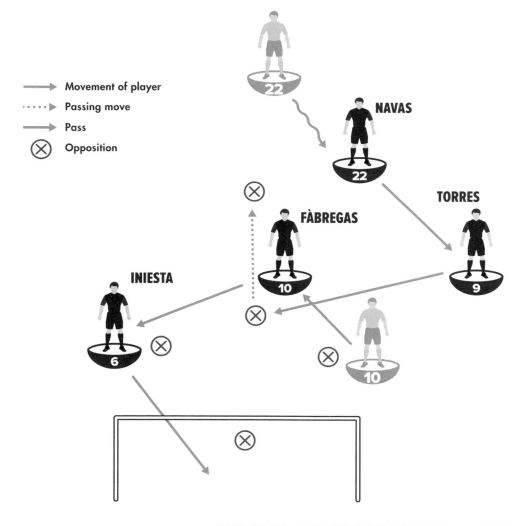

Movement of player

Passing move

Pass

Opposition

NAVAS

TORRES

FÀBREGAS

INIESTA

TIKI TAKA

● ● ● ▶ **Passing moves**

LB

DM

CB

CB

DM

RB

Both matches in this chapter exploited the 'tiki taka' tactic, primarily relying on a short passing style to maintain possession for as much of the game as possible.

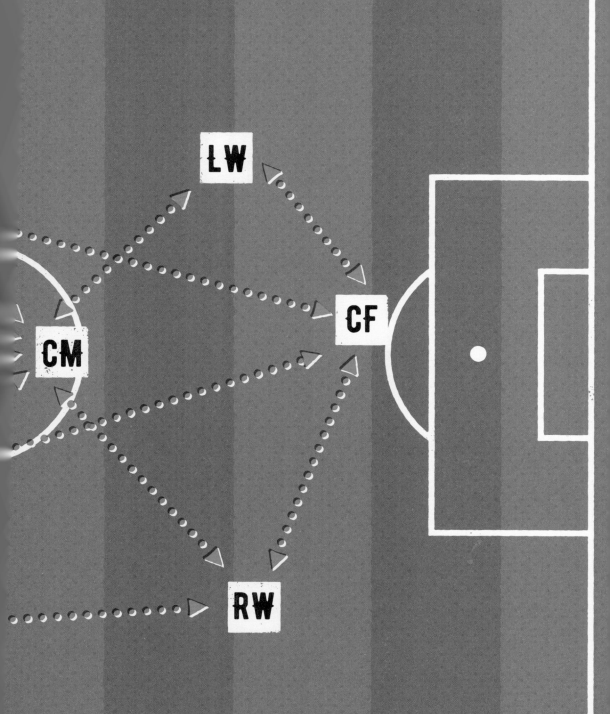

Key Player

In this World Cup Final, the key player was almost certainly Andrés Iniesta, who not only scored the winning goal, but also used his intelligence to play between the lines, with no fixed position. He was able to make space for himself, even when the Netherlands players impressed their physical style during the first forty-five minutes of the game.

towards the goal in a central position. His left-footed shot from twelve yards was deflected wide by the outstretched leg of Iker Casillas. It was possibly the finest save of the Real Madrid player's career. With seven minutes to go, David Villa had an even better chance from maybe six yards out, but his left-footed strike was blocked by the leg of John Heitinga.

In the final ten minutes, Robben raced clear again, but was put off his stride by Carlos Puyol – by fair means and foul – and Casillas was able to prevent it becoming a chance. There were more bookings in the second half – the Netherlands had eight separate players receive yellow cards and, during extra time, Heitinga received a second to become the only man to be sent off in this stunningly physical match. Spain also received three yellow cards during normal time. The sheer number of bookings means the game will not be remembered as the classic it should have been, given all the flair on the pitch.

In extra time, Cesc Fàbregas, a second-half substitute, had a shot saved by Maarten Stekelenburg, while Joris Mathijsen sent a header over the bar when the goal was empty. Fernando Torres was brought on in extra time and a one-two with Andrés Iniesta led to Heitinga committing the foul on Iniesta for which he received his second booking. It was Fàbregas who was involved in the winning goal. He found Iniesta in space inside the penalty area and made a half volley that won the World Cup, the goal scored in the 116th minute.

BARCELONA 5–0 REAL MADRID

LA LIGA, 29 NOVEMBER 2010
CAMP NOU, BARCELONA, ATTENDANCE 98,255

In 2010, Inter Milan may have been European champions, but there was little doubt that the Barcelona team was the one to beat. It had the world's best player in Lionel Messi and had won back-to-back La Liga titles. And they were playing a brand of football that opposition teams were struggling to contain. Possession seemed to be the watchword at the Camp Nou, to such a degree that no less a figure than Zlatan Ibrahimović struggled to hold a place in the side, so attuned to the system were the rest of the players.

When Pep Guardiola took over at Barcelona, he was faced with a team full of talent but that had underachieved for the final two years of Frank Rijkaard's reign. There were rumours of ill discipline and a loss of belief in the coach. Guardiola saw a squad with plenty of talent – there was already the nucleus of the team he would build, with Messi, Xavi, Andrés Iniesta, Victor Valdés and Carles Puyol in the ranks. In time, he would add from within the club players such as Pedro and Sergio Busquets, while re-signing Gerard Piqué, a central defender who had started his career at the Camp Nou before joining Manchester United and spending four years at Old Trafford.

In Guardiola's first season, he won all the prizes available to him, including the league, cup and Champions League treble. In his second year, his team retained the league despite Real Madrid having invested heavily in new players, bringing in Cristiano Ronaldo, Kaka, Karim Benzema and Xabi Alonso during a record-breaking summer of spending. Acting quickly, Barcelona's president Florentino Pérez sacked Manuel Pellegrini after one season, to bring in the most wanted manager in football, José Mourinho. It was this Portuguese coach who had ended Barcelona's Champions League campaign the previous season, his Inter Milan side denying them goal-scoring opportunities at the San Siro and the Camp Nou. There was the added sideline of Mourinho being a previous Barcelona employee – as a translator for Sir Bobby Robson during the Englishman's stint as the Barca manager.

Both teams were already seemingly way out in front at the top of the Primera División. A win for Real would take the team four points clear of its Catalan rivals, while Barca knew a win would see them well on their way to a third successive league title. From a neutral point of view, one wanted to see whether José could once again keep Barca at bay or had last season's Champions League been a fluke? This El Clásico was held on a Monday to give the fixture an even more unique feel. The two sides faced each other an incredible four times more that season, once in the league, a home and away in the Champions League and at the Copa del Rey final. This match had a global audience of over 400 million.

The Match

Messi had already hit the post with a typically impudent effort when Barcelona took the lead in the tenth minute. A pass from the left from Iniesta was intercepted by Marcelo, but the Brazilian was unlucky and his touch fell kindly for the advanced Xavi who hooked the ball past Iker Casillas.

Real threatened on the restart, with Ángel di Maria's shot from outside the penalty area being tipped over the goal by Valdés. Éric Abidal made sure a further attack did not end with Karim Benzema putting the ball into the net after intercepting from five yards out. But soon, the home side doubled their lead. Xavi drifted a pass out to the left where David Villa was lurking and his cross was palmed into the path of Pedro who could not miss in front of an open goal.

The rest of the first half continued in scrappy fashion with both teams being more content to contest decisions and the opposing side's conduct. But it was Barcelona who had most of the ball. Ten minutes into the second half, the third goal came. Barcelona had been enjoying some comfortable possession on the right side when Messi stepped forward and played a short horizontal pass to David Villa, who controlled and shot the ball past an onrushing Casillas.

BARCELONA

GK	1	Victor Valdés
RB	2	Dani Alves
CB	5	Carles Puyol (captain)
CB	3	Gerard Piqué
LB	22	Éric Abidal
CM	6	Xavi
DM	16	Sergio Busquets
CM	8	Andrés Iniesta
RW	17	Pedro
CF	10	Lionel Messi
LW	7	David Villa

Manager Vicente del Bosque

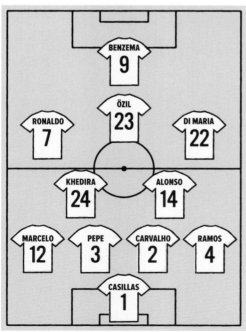

REAL MADRID

GK	1	Iker Casillas (captain)
RB	4	Sergio Ramos
CB	2	Ricardo Carvalho
CB	3	Pepe
LB	12	Marcelo
DM	14	Xabi Alonso
DM	24	Sami Khedira
RW	22	Ángel di Maria
LW	7	Christiano Ronaldo
CM	23	Mesut Özil
CF	9	Karim Benzema

Manager José Mourinho

THE PLAYMAKER

● ● ● ▶ **Passing moves**

CM

DM

CM

Tiki taka was epitomised by Lionel Messi, who played a false 9 role, moving backwards and forwards between the striker and the central midfielders to receive the ball.

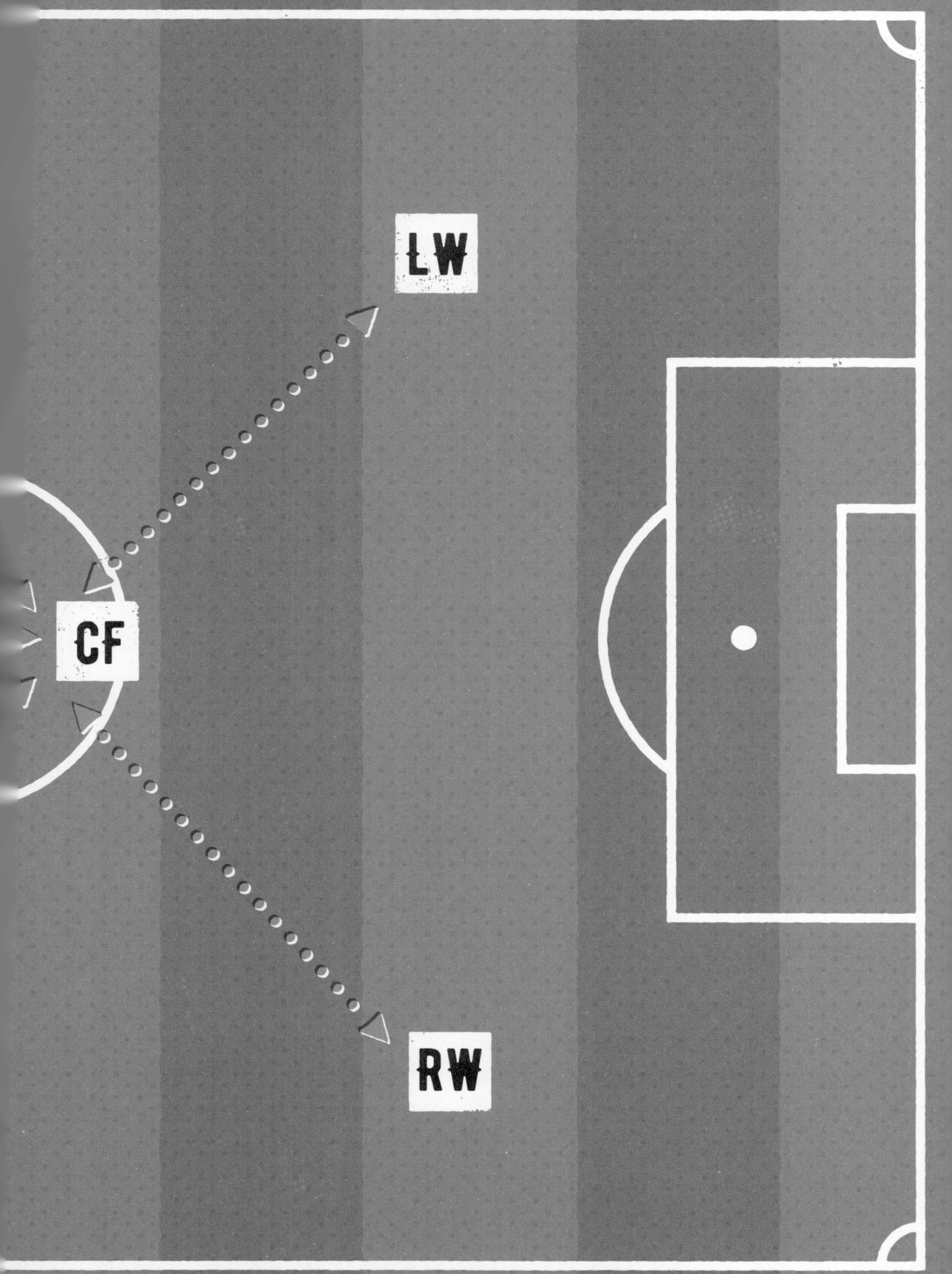
LW
CF
RW

Within two minutes, the lead was extended to four, with the same combination of players wreaking the havoc. Messi picked up the ball on the right side again, this time within his own half and evading the challenges of two defenders before curling a delightful pass into the path of Villa. The striker did not have to break his stride as he slotted the ball under the legs of the oncoming Casillas.

In the first minute of injury time, there was a fifth goal, as a cross was converted by substitute Jeffrén. The strike punctuated what had

On more than one occasion, Messi's unparalled vision led to a Barcelona goal. Here, in the team's third, he split the defence down the middle, enabling Villa to score.

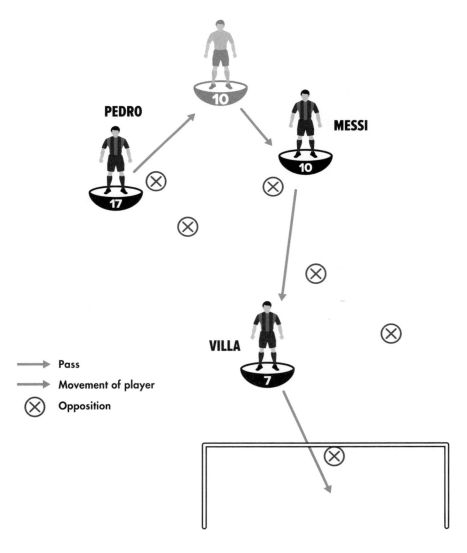

PEDRO

MESSI

VILLA

→ Pass
→ Movement of player
⊗ Opposition

been twenty-five minutes of keeping the ball from the hosts, who did not waste the opportunity to humiliate *los Blancos*. There was still time for Sergio Ramos to receive a straight red card for a scything tackle on Messi, which may have been the closest he had got to the player all night. The statistics do not make pretty reading for Real – Barca had fifteen shots to their five, made 684 passes to their 331 and enjoyed a domination of possession by 67 per cent to 33 per cent.

The last word went to Mourinho, who had this to say after the game: 'One team played very good, one team very bad. Deserved win, deserved loss. Humiliated? No. It's easy to deal with this loss, we just weren't good enough.' Barcelona went on to win the Spanish and Champions leagues that season, with the Copa del Rey the consolation for Real.

The Philosophy

It seems strange, yet fair, to compare these two games in one philosophy. The games are from different competitions, one involving an international side, the other a club team. But there is one phrase that can be used to describe the football of both Spain and Barcelona: tiki taka. The phrase derives from a particular Spanish TV commentary on a football match from the mid-2000s. Many people say the tactic took root during the stewardship of Johan Cruyff at Barcelona, when he fashioned the dream team. The key characteristic of the side is an adherence to a short passing style that is designed specifically to

THREE AT
THE BACK

LB

CB

CB

RE

Range of movement

Passing moves

Frequently, one of Barcelona's full backs would advance to make better use of the tactic's short passing style midfield.

keep possession of the ball. In the majority of matches, this allowed the side, be it Spain or Barcelona, to keep the ball for up to 70 per cent of the time.

The Frenchman Thierry Henry, who played in Barcelona's 2008–09 vintage, said that Guardiola wanted his players to retain their positions as much as possible, until they reached the final third of the pitch. It was there that players were encouraged to visit their individuality and try to create or score goals. One other thing that both Guardiola and Cruyff believed in, was that the style of play should not be impeded by the willingness to keep the ball and not move forward. Guardiola once said he hated tiki taka and passing for the sake of passing; Cruyff also opined that he preferred goals scored with minimal effort and maximum efficiency.

If both claim that dislike of passing for the sake of passing, then it must be pointed out that possession of the ball is one way to defend, and that retention of the ball gives the opposition the problem of having to win back the football and expose its own defensive shape. It is at that moment that Spain/Barcelona can strike. One of the key differences between the two sides was Lionel Messi. Spain did not have a similar player in their line-up and, instead, David Villa played a central role, flanked by the running of Pedro and prompting of Andrés Iniesta. For Barcelona, Messi's game intelligence allowed his team's game to remain fluid. There is no accounting for this – the Argentine's positional sense, the way the ball seemed attracted to him, meant his side never lost shape, even though he was allowed freedom within a fairly strict team dynamic. Guardiola knew from the end of his first season as coach that a system designed to suit the player would pay huge dividends for his side. Tiki taka thus became the system in which the false 9 flourished.

Other differences between the two sides lay in their formation and deployment of players. For Barcelona, Iniésta played in a central midfield of three, with his long-time teammate, Xavi, and Sergio Busquets. Here, Xavi and Busquets shared defensive responsibility, with the latter more likely to remain fixed in his patrolling areas. For Spain, Busquets was often paired with Xabi Alonso or Cesc Fàbregas and Xavi was pushed forward ahead of those two, even though his career stats do not suggest he is much of a goal threat.

The question that must be posed is why the system seemed to work so effectively? In terms of the Spanish national side, generations of players were used to adhering to a system similar to the one the national side used, even if their club teams didn't adopt it. What made the system work better was the use of dynamic full backs who were able to exploit the space made by the possession superiority: with the opposition trying to win back the ball infield, Sergio Ramos and Joan Capdevila had enough pace to find space, unmarked, on the wings and so drive the ball forward. For Barcelona, these places were occupied by Dani Alves and Éric Abidal, intelligent players who could make the runs at the right time.

What really worked well for Barca in the Real game was the team's ability to maintain possession midfield, with Real chasing the ball thirty or forty yards from their own goal. In those circumstances, Messi, with his brilliance, speed and insight, could more easily pass a long ball to Villa, unmarked on the wing, when the right moment struck. He did so several times and not just for the two goals. Real's midfield lacked the ball winner who could spend his evening tracking Messi. In Sami Khedira and Xabi Alonso, Mourinho didn't have the players who could fulfil that role.

One other thing to note is the Barcelona starting line-up. Eight of them had come through the Barcelona academy La Masia and had been trained with the ideals put down by Johan Cruyff. What would have pleased Cruyff was how four of the goals came through swift, direct passing. It was perhaps closer to total football as practised by the Dutch in the 1970s. For del Bosque, he articulated his ethos to FIFA's official website a few months after the triumph:

'With the midfielders we've got it's impossible to play anything other than a possession game and mix long balls up with short ones. We have our strong points and we can't go against them, but no team is complete without having some defensive strengths too. In our case that's our ability to close the opposition down and win the ball back.'

10

GERMANY
RECLAIMS
THE THRONE

THE MATCH

GERMANY 7–1 BRAZIL

World Cup Semi-Final
8 July 2014
Estadio Mineirão, Belo Horizonte, Brazil

GERMANY RECLAIMS THE THRONE

If there was ever a suspicion that Spain or Barcelona would meet a kryptonite version of their football style, the first hints that such a thing existed appeared during a two-leg Champions League tie in 2013. Barcelona, who had won two of the last four Champions League titles, faced Bayern Munich, defeated finalists of 2012. The result was a 7–0 aggregate victory to the German side, including a 3–0 win at a silenced Camp Nou. The German side seemed too quick and powerful for the soon-to-be crowned Spanish champions.

GERMANY 7–1 BRAZIL

WORLD CUP SEMI-FINAL, 8 JULY 2014
ESTADIO MINEIRÃO, BELO HORIZONTE, ATTENDANCE 58,141

If that result didn't alert experts to the fact that there was about to be a massive shift in the footballing landscape, the World Cup of 2014 would do. Argentina versus the Netherlands provided a semi-final ultimately decided by penalties in favour of the former, but in the other game, a Brazil side that had been inspired by Neymar faced

GERMANY

GK	1	Manuel Neuer
RB	16	Philipp Lahm (captain)
CB	20	Jérôme Boateng
CB	5	Mats Hummels
LB	4	Benedikt Höwedes
CM	6	Sami Khedira
CM	7	Bastian Schweinsteiger
RW	13	Thomas Müller
AM	18	Toni Kroos
LW	8	Mesut Özil
CF	11	Miroslav Klose

Manager Joachim Löw

BRAZIL

GK	12	Júlio César
RB	23	Maicon
CB	4	David Luiz (captain)
CB	13	Dante
LB	6	Marcelo
CM	17	Luiz Gustavo
CM	5	Fernandinho
RW	7	Hulk
AM	11	Oscar
LW	20	Bernard
CF	9	Fred

Manager Luiz Felipe Scolari

Germany, who had once again reached the last four of a major tournament. Incredibly, though, the Germans' last triumph at a major international tournament had been in 1996.

The team's route to this stage had been curiously underwhelming. After beating Portugal 4–0 in their first game, they drew 2–2 with Ghana, before scraping a 1–0 victory over the USA. A last-sixteen match against Algeria, in which extra time was required before they could score, seemed to add more weight to the notion that this Germany team struggled to be as efficient as previous sides. A narrow 1–0 victory over France saw the team take its place in the last four and the real good news for them was that Neymar was out of the semi with injury and Brazil's best defender, Thiago Silva, was suspended. However, history was on the side of the hosts playing in Belo Horizonte. Brazil hadn't lost a competitive match at home for thirty-nine years. There had been worries before the tournament started about how the Brazil team would fare without Neymar and Silva, but those doubts were assuaged when the side beat Colombia comfortably in the quarter-final a few days earlier.

What should have worried Brazil was the continuity in the German side. Five of its players came from the Bayern Munich team that had won the Champions League 14 months earlier and many of them had been part of the squad that reached the last four in South Africa at the last World Cup. They were fast becoming known as the golden generation of German footballers – so skilled were they, that players of such high calibre as André Schürrle, Mario Götze and Julian Draxler found themselves on the bench.

The Match

Football matches last for at least ninety minutes, but this game was defined by an extraordinary first half an hour. In their game against France, Germany had taken an early lead and had been able to retain it for the rest of the game. There was the feeling they would be able to do so again in this match against Brazil, when Thomas Müller struck in the eleventh minute, with a volley from an unmarked position just outside the six-yard box.

Twelve minutes later, Germany doubled their lead. Toni Kroos was able to slip a ball into the path of Müller, who spotted Miroslav Klose running in the opposite direction. The striker converted on his second attempt to become the all-time leading scorer in World Cups. One minute later, Kroos added a third goal, when Philipp Lahm's cross was missed by Brazil defenders, and Kroos volleyed the ball past Júlio César. Within ninety seconds, the midfielder had added a fourth. He dispossessed Fernandinho thirty yards from goal and then played an economic one-two with Sami Khedira before slotting home. Khedira was the next to get in on the act. Again, the move started with Brazil losing the ball in the defensive midfield area, and

With Sami Khedira moving forward to create a four-man midfield, and Müller and Özil ready to come in from the wings, Germany were formidable on the attack.

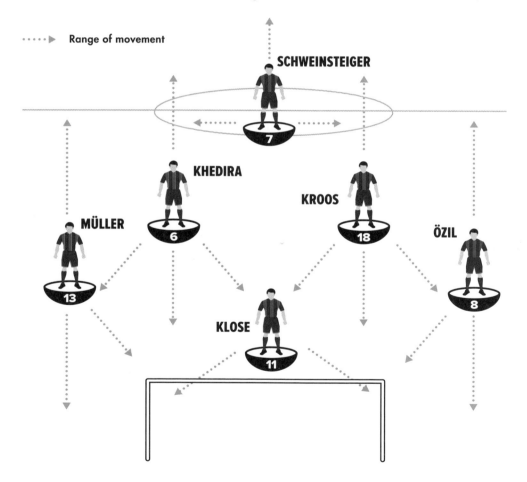

Range of movement

SCHWEINSTEIGER
7

KHEDIRA
6

KROOS
18

MÜLLER
13

ÖZIL
8

KLOSE
11

QUICK CHANGE

●●●▶ **Range of movement**

LB

CB

GK

CB

CM

RB

Germany's 4–2–3–1 formation rapidly changed to a 4–1–4–1 on the attack, but could revert easily to create a two-man midfield when defending.

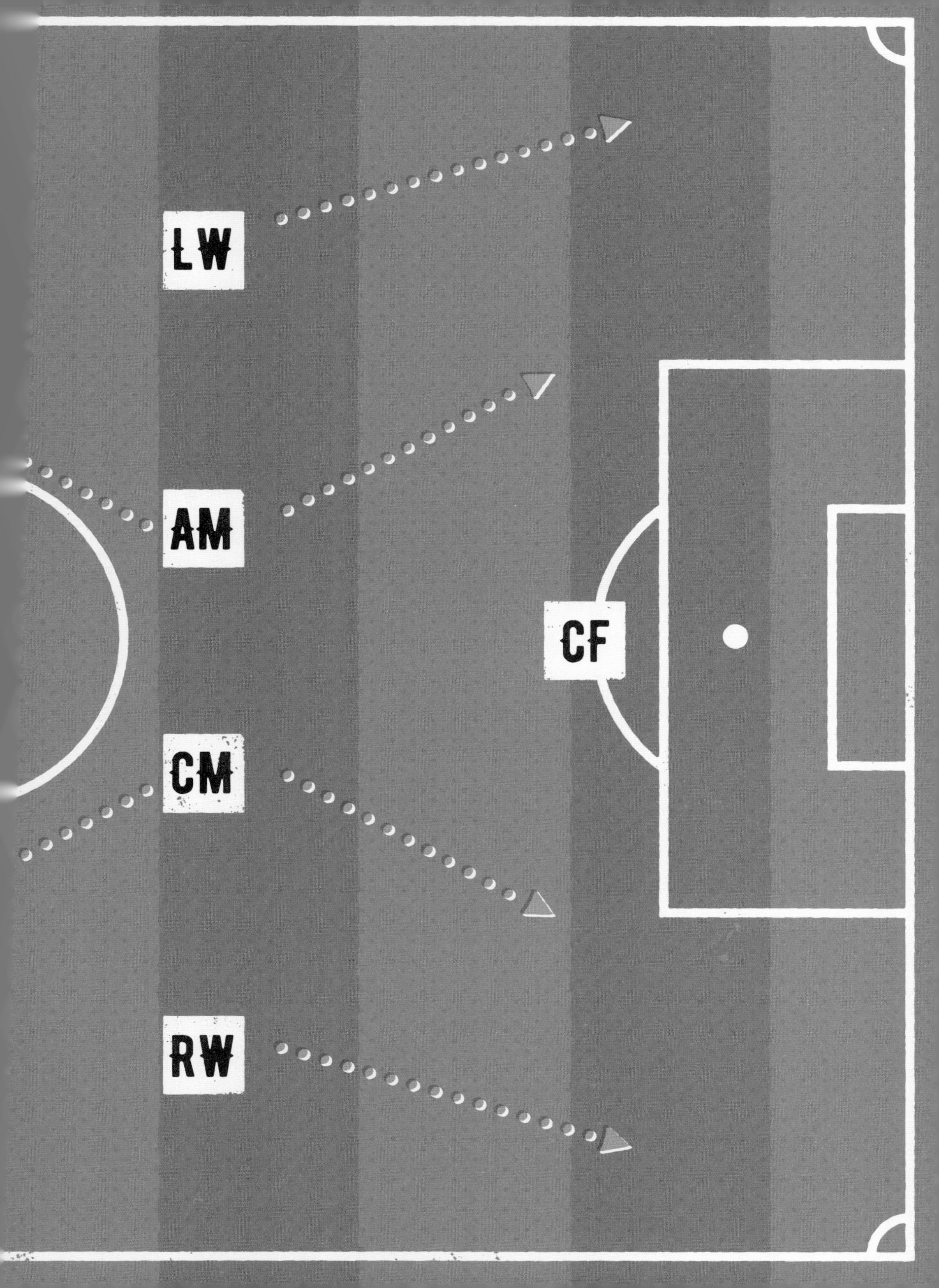
LW
AM
CF
CM
RW

Khedira driving the ball past a hopelessly exposed César after Mesut Özil drew out the keeper.

Already, there were tears among the Brazil faithful, who could not have expected anything remotely like this. The last four goals had been scored in a shockingly brutal phase of play that lasted just six minutes. The game was over and there was still an hour of action remaining. Another forty minutes of action took place, during which time Brazil threatened a consolation, but found that Manuel Neuer, perhaps the best keeper in the world, was equal to anything they could throw at him. He made reflex saves to deny both Oscar

Germany's fourth goal demonstrates how Germany were able to dupe Brazil's defence time and again.

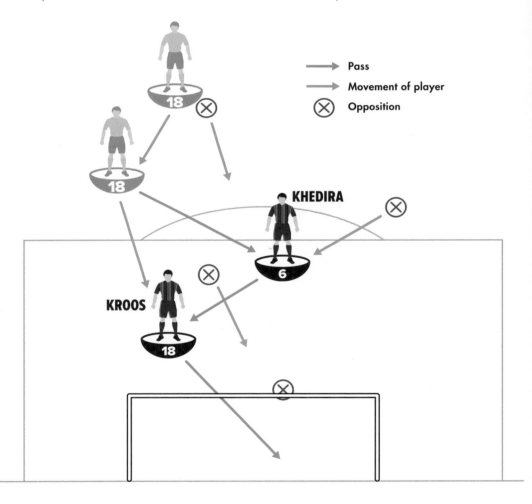

Pass

Movement of player

⊗ Opposition

KHEDIRA

KROOS

and a substitute, Paulinho. A sixth goal was added when André Schürrle, who had replaced Klose, took a pass from captain Lahm, who had drifted infield and, in keeping with many of the finishes, calmly stroked the ball into the net. It was Schürrle who scored the seventh, and best, individual goal of the evening. Müller had pulled the Brazil defence to the left side of the pitch and his lobbed lay off found Schürrle with time to measure a half volley that soared into the net, past the hapless César.

Neuer's sweeper-keeper role had prevented Brazil from any counter-attacks but he was helpless in the final minute, when Oscar ran through and calmly buried a finish into the corner of the net. It was hard not to have some sympathy for the Brazil manager, Luis Felipe Scolari, who resigned at the end of the tournament. Germany went on to win the final against Argentina, though they needed an extra-time goal from Mario Götze to do it.

'Who is responsible? Who is responsible for picking the team? I am. It's me. So the catastrophic result can be shared by the whole group, and my players will tell you we will share our responsibilities, but who decided the tactics? I did. So the person responsible is me. I did what I thought was best.' *Luis Felipe Scolari.*

The Philosophy

Both sides operated with back fours, with Brazil starting with two holding central midfielders. Ahead of them were three attacking midfielders with one central striker in Fred. Germany had a similar set-up that changed readily to a 4–1–4–1 line-up, with Bastian Schweinsteiger as a holding midfielder, and Khedira and Kroos forming part of an attacking four when in offence and withdrawing into a midfield three when defending.

What Germany did after the first goal was to make the game a compact affair. They were helped with that by Brazil's distribution from the back frequently missing the target.

Although Brazil had more of the ball, they were so wasteful in possession that they gave the impression of a side that was ready to

EXPLOITING THE DEFENCE

■	Germany
●	Brazil
•••▶	Range of movement

CM

Brazil frequently left a two-man defence to man-mark Özil and Klose, leaving gaps in the midfield for Kloos, Müller and Khedira.

RB

LW   CB

CF   GK

RW   CB

ŁB

be taken apart. While the modern vogue is to talk about the pressing game that has been made popular by Bayern Munich and Borussia Dortmund, Germany were smart enough not to show their teeth until the twentieth minute, when they realised they had nothing to fear from Brazil. John Bennett, who was covering the game in Belo Horizonte for the BBC, says that Brazil did not help themselves during that incredible passage of play and that Germany went up a level: 'The one difference for Germany at this World Cup was they absolutely went for the kill. In previous years, they might have sat back after taking the lead, wary that Brazil might hit them on the break.'

Of the five goals that the Germans scored before half-time, the majority came from the team squeezing the Brazil defence and starving it of room. Although Khedira and Kroos were supposed to be acting as screens for their defence, both spent ten minutes harrying Fernandinho and Luiz Gustavo before starting swift counter-attacks. Germany had practised the art of swift finishes and scoring goals in a handful of seconds.

Germany were able to push high because of their faith in keeper Neuer, who was redefining the role of a stopper who plays as an auxillary sweeper. At the other end, Brazil's ageing keeper tended to patrol his six-yard box and exposed his defence whenever he did leave his line, because he lacked the pace to challenge Germany's attackers. Conscious of this, David Luiz and Dante did not move forward with their full backs and found themselves isolated when Germany pressed. In this way, Müller and Özil were able to advance towards goal with Marcelo and Maicon out of position, both of them expecting passes that never came. Once the game had been won with those first five goals, Germany did not press as high; the need for further strikes wasn't as great. So Schweinsteiger became more relevant as the man who dictated the tempo of Germany's play, seeking the early pass to and from his teammates. Germany compressed their shape, with Kroos and Khedira playing closer to their defence, leaving Müller to work as a lone striker, once Klose was taken off midway through the second half.

The approach wasn't a merciful one, as evidenced by Schürrle scoring twice in the second half. On both occasions, Germany was able to exploit the uncertainty between Brazil's centre backs and full backs. While most back fours tend to play narrower when under attack, the massive gaps in the Brazil defence were still apparent. Or, to put it another way, when the Brazil left was under attack, the defenders did not shift across to help out a teammate – they played as individuals operating in their own zones, and not moving as a unit.

Analysing the many problems faced by Brazil's chaotic organisation is to do a disservice to the precision of Germany's play. Their attacks were rarely self-indulgent, but focused on the quickest and most efficient way to get the ball into the net. And the team withstood Brazilian attempts to press, simply by holding its shape and asking Khedira and Kroos to win the ball back and leave the host team in disarray. A final word of caution to sound for Germany is the potential to expose the high line that their defence kept. It was owing to this that Oscar scored his consolation goal and it was the way Argentina nearly beat them in the final, with Lionel Messi and Gonzalo Higuaín almost exposing them on two occasions. Genuine pace, such as that which Neymar could have offered, was missing from the Brazilian line-up and might be something to use in future when other teams play Germany.

11

THE RETURN OF THE THREE

THE MATCH

MANCHESTER CITY 1–3 CHELSEA

Premier League
3 December 2016
Etihad Stadium, Manchester, England

THE RETURN OF THE THREE

This game was a match-up between the league leaders (Chelsea) and a side assembled at huge cost under the most sought-after manager in European football (Manchester City and Pep Guardiola, respectively). Chelsea approached the game having won seven consecutive matches in the Premier League.

MANCHESTER CITY 1-3 CHELSEA

PREMIER LEAGUE, 3 DECEMBER 2016
ETIHAD STADIUM, MANCHESTER, ATTENDANCE 54,457

Chelsea's manager, Antonio Conte, decided to revert to a back-three formation, which had served him well as Juventus coach and, subsequently, as Italy's manager. On this occasion, City also went with a back three, with Guardiola in search of the formula that had helped his team start the season in such imperious style. For him, defensive solidity had always been based on ball retention and starving the opposition of possession. John Stones played as the central man, with Nicolás Otamendi and Aleksandar Kolarov either side.

So far that season, City had kept just one clean sheet at home, seemingly still trying to come to terms with Guardiola's tactics. Chief among those was for the centre backs to split when in possession,

MANCHESTER CITY

GK	1	Claudio Bravo
DF	30	Nicolás Otamendi
DF	24	John Stones
DF	11	Aleksandar Kolarov
MF	15	Jésus Navas
MF	25	Fernandinho
MF	8	Ilkay Gündogan
MF	19	Leroy Sané
FW	17	Kevin De Bruyne
FW	21	David Silva (captain)
FW	10	Sergio Agüero

Manager Pep Guardiola

CHELSEA

GK	13	Thibaut Courtois
DF	28	César Azpilicueta
DF	30	David Luiz
DF	24	Gary Cahill (captain)
MF	15	Victor Moses
MF	7	N'Golo Kanté
MF	4	Cesc Fàbregas
MF	3	Marcos Alonso
FW	11	Pedro
FW	19	Diego Costa
FW	10	Eden Hazard

Manager Antonio Conte

with a central midfielder sitting in the middle. For this game, the team had a strong central midfield with Fernandinho, Ilkay Gündogan and Kevin De Bruyne offering protection to the back three. The back-three system had largely been shunned by teams in the top half of the table for many years. It was viewed, rightly or wrongly, as unnecessarily cautious and defensive.

Conte made no changes to his favoured formation for this fixture. He was comfortable with his wingbacks facing up to the pace and trickery of Jésus Navas and Leroy Sané. A win for City would have taken them back to the top, while a Chelsea victory would extend the side's lead over the Manchester club by four points. Both clubs were fielding their star strikers on the day – Sergio Agüero for City and Diego Costa for Chelsea.

The Match

Guardiola's teams had generally dominated possession during his time at Barcelona, Bayern Munich and now, at Manchester City. They averaged 55 to 60 per cent of the ball and Guardiola expected that average to be maintained against this Chelsea.

With Chelsea reverting to a back five when not in possession of the ball, space on the pitch was tight and, for the first forty-five minutes, it was not easy for Guardiola's side to break through. Most chances occurred when either side went direct. Agüero tested Thibaut Courtois's reflexes with a shot from outside the area, while Eden Hazard went around City keeper Claudio Bravo, but his ball back into the area was cleared by City. There were also signs throughout the half that, if Chelsea could break through the trickery and pace of Hazard, they had a real chance of hurting City, who seemed disorganised at the back.

As the half drew to a close, City came even closer – a ball over the visitors' defence saw Sané cross the ball for Agüero. But Agüero's turn and swivel was blocked by the body of César Azpilicueta. Agüero had another chance shortly after, but he headed wide after De Bruyne crossed with real pace. In first-half injury time, finally, City took the lead when Gary Cahill turned a Navas cross into his own net.

The home side should have extended its lead at the start of the second half – Agüero missed another chance and De Bruyne had two opportunities to score, the second with an open goal, which he missed from around six yards. Such extravagance was always likely to be punished by a team that was destined to become champions. Sure enough, on the hour, Cesc Fàbregas found Costa with a lofted through ball and the Brazilian-born striker brought the ball down inside the City area to drive a finish past Bravo.

Rigorous man-to-man marking by Cahill and Azpilicueta left Luiz free to roam.

· · · · · ▶ **Range of movement**

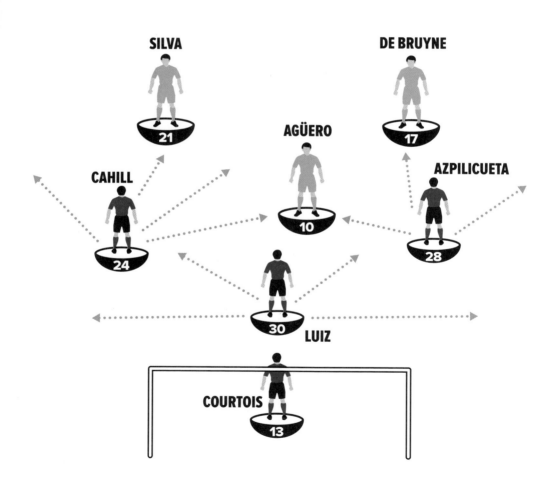

A VERSATILE FORMATION

····▶ Range of movement

MF

DF

DF

GK

MF

DF

MF

Conte's 3–4–3 formation could easily revert to 5–3–2 in a defending situation, with David Luiz acting as sweeper.

FW

FW

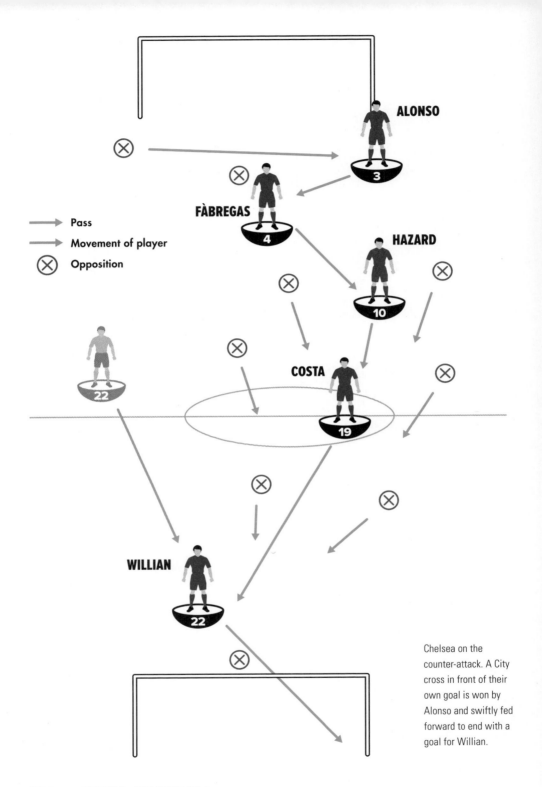

ALONSO

FÀBREGAS

HAZARD

COSTA

WILLIAN

→ Pass

→ Movement of player

⊗ Opposition

Chelsea on the counter-attack. A City cross in front of their own goal is won by Alonso and swiftly fed forward to end with a goal for Willian.

Ten minutes later, Chelsea were in the lead. After surviving another frantic scramble in its own area, Conte's side broke quickly again and a substitute, Willian, was able to run directly at the City goal before hitting a hard and low shot past Bravo. For all their dominance in terms of chances created, City looked vulnerable as soon as their attacks were repelled and Chelsea started to counter. While the visitors were able to get bodies in the way to create a sense of panic when City attacked, they were also poised when they had the opportunity to create chances of their own.

This characteristic of the Chelsea side was epitomised when Hazard scored a third goal in the final minute, running clear of the home side's defence and making the finish past Bravo look very simple. A melee ensued at the end of the match, in which both Agüero and Fernandinho were sent off. In months to come, this was remembered as the day on which Chelsea showed their title credentials and Guardiola realised what he needed to do if he was going to build a title-winning side in England.

The Philosophy

Playing three at the back is normally interpreted as a defensive formation, because it encourages the team ultimately to defend with five – the wing backs holding a line along with the other defenders. But Conte had been using the three at the back for a while and was able to instruct his side in the merits of such a system.

One of the biggest differences with this system was his ability to get players to work to his orders. The player with the greatest responsibility here was David Luiz, who played at the centre of Chelsea's back three. Luiz had always been regarded as an incredibly talented player, yet some thought he lacked the discipline to play a key role in defence. Conte did not hold this view, however, and had given Luiz instructions always to work as the spare man. In the first half, he frequently put himself in the centre to stop crosses from the right or sometimes left.

The three at the back works well with a player like Luiz to fill that sweeper role and with Luiz's substantial gifts – shooting, passing and

SWIFT COUNTER-ATTACK

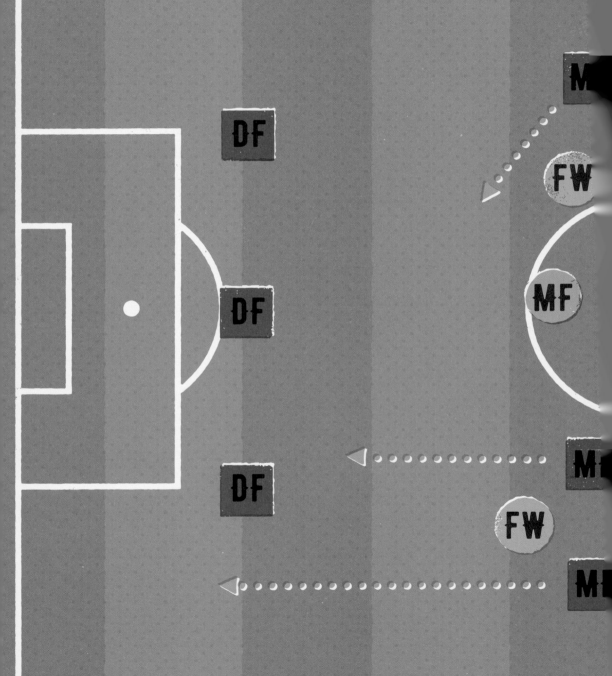

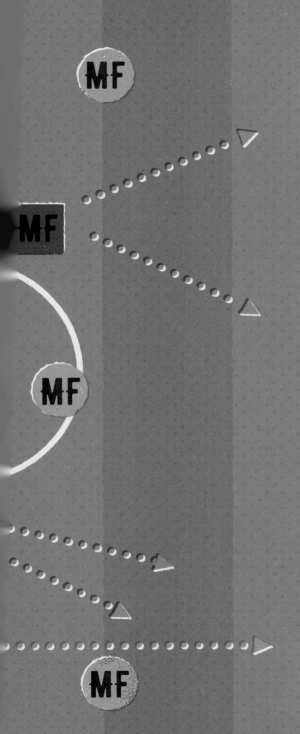

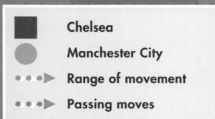

■	**Chelsea**
●	**Manchester City**
●●●▶	**Range of movement**
●●●▶	**Passing moves**

Keeping three at the back allowed for an extra player to maintain pressure midfield, making swift counter-attacks easier to effect.

Key Player

While Eden Hazard was instrumental in the victory, with his smart movement and the ability to take the ball from his defence and begin a swift attack, Conte's system functioned so well because of the diligence of David Luiz. The Brazilian was strong when he needed to be and alert when it mattered. Although he had aspirations to play midfield, he was a revelation for Chelsea in this game and throughout the season in defence. Across world football, it is becoming increasingly difficult to find players who can adapt to the sweeper role. With his speed and eye for a pass, he was the right man at the right time that season.

speed – if his best could be harnessed, he could play an instrumental role. But there is another reason for a team to adopt the three-at-the-back formation, according to broadcaster Hugh Ferris, who was at the Etihad Stadium that Saturday:

'Conte used three at the back to free up Eden Hazard, because Hazard was always having to play with some form of responsibility. Playing three at the back allows you to free up another attacker, whether it is a striker or a player like Hazard. A lot of people wrongly say that playing three at the back is a defensive ploy.'

Ferris also says that Conte was able to implement the new system because, for the first time in years, Chelsea did not have to worry about a Champions League midweek game because they weren't in the competition. This allowed the Italian time to work on his desired formation on the training ground. It also helped that he had good players to work with.

The other way that Conte was allowed to make his system work was in the centre of his midfield. He arrived knowing that the intelligent prompting and experienced head of Cesc Fàbregas was at his disposal, while in N'Golo Kanté, he had a man who could hassle the lives of any attackers. It meant that the ball could be won back quickly using a sophisticated pressing system that relied on the fitness of Kanté, with the ball then recycled efficiently through the expert vision of Fàbregas, whose long passes were suited to the direct running of Costa and pace of Hazard.

The core philosophy of Conte's football tactics is built around organisation and hard work. The Italian was renowned, when he was national manager, for picking sides that suited his system rather than attempting to fit in all the most talented players. His 3–4–3 could also become 5–3–2 if needed, to make crossing difficult. Conte's sides would press through the middle, almost inviting the opposition players to go wide and try their luck from full backs or through wingers. His defensive organisation can be attributed to his upbringing in Serie A, where solidity is as important as any other quality. But what he does do going forward is maximise possession through a fast dribbler (Hazard) and a central striker (Costa in his title-winning side and, in the 2017–18 season, Álvaro Morata).

Of course, the opposition will eventually find a way through the congestion of the centre and at that stage, the central defender is required to go as tight as possible and force the attacker to restart the attack with a backward pass. The three at the back and, with it, the release of another attacking midfielder, has been adopted by other leading sides in the Premier League in recent years. Arsenal and Tottenham Hotspur started using it in the 2016–17 season and both Manchester United and Liverpool have used it when opposing teams have planned very defensive strategies.

INDEX

ACKNOWLEDGEMENTS

Even with my fifth decade of life nearing its end, I still consider a day spent talking about football time well used. Fortunately, other people share this belief. So thanks very much to the following, who took the time to share their thoughts with me: Jonathan Stevenson, Gergely Marcosi, Adnan Nawaz, Mina Rzouki, Phil Ball, Tom van Hulsen, Tim Vickery, Graham Turner, Loïc Tanzi, Hugh Ferris, John Bennett and Steven Wyeth. Be assured that if you find value in this text, their opinions and knowledge made this work a lot better.

Owing to constraints of space, it is impossible for me to list the hundreds of articles that I have accessed in putting this book together, so let me just credit the *Guardian*, FIFA, UEFA, *Daily Mail*, Outside of the Boot, Hard Tackle, These Football Times, The False 9, Bleacher Report, *The Blizzard*, *FourFourTwo*, AjaxDaily, the *Independent*, the *Liverpool Echo*, Spielverlagerung, Squawka Football, Zonal Marking, goal.com and various other blogs that have provided valuable instruction and direction.

This is the third book I have worked on with Aurum and Lucy Warburton, whose determination and encouragement made the project possible. And I'm not being nice just because she is my editor. Gratitude also goes to Anna Southgate, who was with me every step of the way in terms of thoughts and guidance, and Jack Phillips, for his invaluable advice illustrating the tactics. A special word goes to Alison Anderson for her meticulous proofing. Speaking of wonderful, I struggle to find the right words to say thank you to Laura Clays, my wife of a few years who let me get on with the job of writing this book while there was a house to run and children to raise.

It occurs to me that I often use these words at the end of a book to pay homage to someone who is no longer with us. So let me instead choose to say thank you to my father, very much alive, and whose love and support got me this far. Thanks Dad.

BIBLIOGRAPHY

My Turn: The Autobiography, Johan Cruyff, Pan MacMillan

The Mixer: The Story of Premier League Tactics from Route One to False Nines, Michael Cox, HarperCollins

Managing My Life: My Autobiography, Sir Alex Ferguson with Hugh McIlvanney, Hodder and Stoughton

Das Reboot: How German Football Reinvented Itself, Raphael Honigstein, Yellow Jersey Press

Barca: The Making of the Greatest Team in the World, Graham Hunter, BackPage Press

McIlvanney on Football, Hugh McIlvanney, Mainstream Publishing

Inverting the Pyramid: The History of Football Tactics, Jonathan Wilson, Orion